Flawless, My Dear

DUCHESS WIBBERFLUFFLE

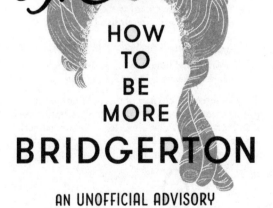

Flawless, My Dear

HOW TO BE MORE
BRIDGERTON

AN UNOFFICIAL ADVISORY

HarperCollins*Publishers*

HarperCollins*Publishers*
1 London Bridge Street
London SE1 9GF

www.harpercollins.co.uk

HarperCollins*Publishers*
1st Floor, Watermarque Building, Ringsend Road
Dublin 4, Ireland

First published by HarperCollins*Publishers* 2021

1 3 5 7 9 10 8 6 4 2

© HarperCollins*Publishers* 2021

Illustrations © Ollie Mann

Tamsin English asserts the moral right to
be identified as the author of this work

A catalogue record of this book is
available from the British Library

ISBN 978-0-00-849111-6

Printed and bound in Great Britain by
CPI Group (UK) Ltd, Croydon

All rights reserved. No part of this publication may be
reproduced, stored in a retrieval system, or transmitted,
in any form or by any means, electronic, mechanical,
photocopying, recording or otherwise, without the
prior written permission of the publishers.

MIX
Paper from
responsible sources
FSC™ C007454

This book is produced from independently certified FSC™ paper
to ensure responsible forest management.

For more information visit: www.harpercollins.co.uk/green

To all the ladies out there who are so
desperately in need of instruction.

CONTENTS

ABOUT THE AUTHOR

Duchess Wibberfluffle is the author of several explosive society papers and this book. It is certain that her moniker is a pseudonym, which many an amateur sleuth has been attempting to uncover in a very half-hearted and ladylike way. Top contenders for the REAL Duchess Wibberfluffle include Bristol-based author Tamsin English, HRH the Duchess of Cornwall, Stephen Fry and Kylie Jenner.

INTRODUCTION

YOU ARE CORDIALLY INVITED TO YOUR DEBUT SEASON

Dearest reader,

First and foremost, may I congratulate you on picking up this high-society handbook – you have excellent taste. This good judgement will stand you in good stead as you take your place in society during this, your opening season. Your sole aim, dear debutante: find a husband and make a match that will enrapture the Ton.

Do not be daunted, for I will clutch your elegant gloved hand and guide you through the triumphs and tribulations of this testing time. There is much work to be done, gentle reader, to ensure that you are not merely marriage material (in your current state, you simply will

not do), but that you will shine above all others as a sparkling gem this season. Remember, your future happiness hinges on enticing a dashing gentleman of noble rank.

Allow me to teach you how to be charming in the presence of suitors, to divulge a few simple tricks to ensure your bod is ballroom-ready (spoiler: eat nothing!) and how to squeeze your mighty bosom into an alluring empire-line gown. In addition, I shall impart the most direct way to make an impact with one's embroidery; how to fend off the gropes of a rake; how to be a girl-boss in what may seem like a man's world; the secret science behind finding your perfect match (and possibly even love); insights into the mysterious 'marital act'; tips for flaunting your pantaloons on honeymoon to drive your groom wild; and how to survive birthing an heir. All this and sumptuous recipes for Cook to prepare, as well as some parlour games, quizzes and more to play with your chums.

Along the way, we will observe some triumphs of the season and also some shocking faux pas – cautionary tales of how some debutantes can be ruined by careless breaches in decorum.

Dearest reader, forget what you think you know about husband-hunting, and abandon your friends if you must, for within these very pages you will discover all you need to know to be the diamond of the season.

Yours,

Duchess Wibberfluffle

1

DEBUTANTE SOCIAL ETIQUETTE: SPEAK LITTLE, SPIN WELL

Welcome to your first season, my dears – is there anything more thrilling than making one's debut in society? Balls, gowns, gossip and scandal – what a time you will have! But I must warn you, it's not all fun and games. Your future happiness hinges on the success of your demeanour, because one false move – a curtsy that's not quite low enough, your silk gloves falling below your elbows (saucy minx!) or, heaven forfend, you find yourself momentarily unchaperoned in the company of a gentleman – and your prospects on the marriage market will diminish faster than the Queen's tin of snuff.

So, follow these failsafe protocols and not only will you survive your first season unscathed; you will become its most sparkling diamond – the incomparable debutante of the season.

HOW TO BECOME THE JEWEL OF THE SEASON

Looking resplendent is non-negotiable. All eyes will be on you. There are detailed chapters in this guide dedicated to this – turn to pages 21 and 35 forthwith if this is your biggest challenge – because such is the importance of your allure. While the otherwise repugnant Lord Berbrooke may favour a lady's accomplishments over beauty, we cannot expect such an enlightened view from every gentleman. Your beauty must appear nonchalant and effortless (though there will have been many hours of effort put into it. Obviously). This is the time to increase the frequency of your bi-monthly bathe to monthly, break out the Castile soap and have your maid groom you into the prize filly that you are. As a sidenote: the orientation of your cleavage is crucial, and its deliberate arrangement on any given evening will serve to impart coded messages to your suitors (see page 40 for more).

Think no more of Miss Penelope Featherington's lacklustre approach to social occasions. It's not enough to simply bear your first season; instead you must aim to thrive – dreary defeatism just won't do. This must be your first and your last season (if you are yet to become engaged by nineteen, you are practically a spinster). There's no greater dejection than having to file out season after season, on the shelf for all to see, then eventually be married off to some hairy, ageing, gout-ridden widower who has already impregnated his dish wench.

Let us remember the three Ps:

POSTURE: If you can breathe comfortably, something is wrong. Your ribs and internal organs need urgent compression – visit your modiste immediately.

POISE: Remain enchanting and agreeable at all times. Stifle that yawn, ignore the intruding petticoat digging into your undercarriage. A lady must appear serene even in the most disagreeable of circumstances.

POMERANIANS: Winning favour with the sovereign's hounds is everything. Displease your queen and it's a one-stop train to old maid town.

THE GENTLEMAN: WHAT IS IT AND HOW DOES ONE CONVERSE WITH IT?

Until this, your first season, you may have only encountered these creatures peripherally – that is to say, you've never actually met one in the wild. Yes, you have heard tell of their existence, perhaps even seen one in the

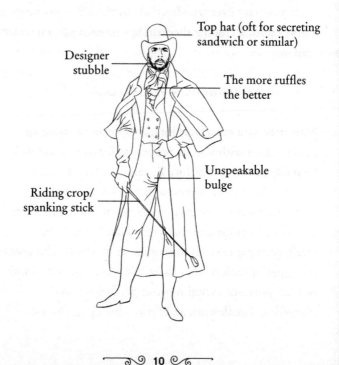

Top hat (oft for secreting sandwich or similar)

Designer stubble

The more ruffles the better

Unspeakable bulge

Riding crop/ spanking stick

distance at a jolly picnic at your family's ancestral home in the country, and you may even have a father or brother (who do, technically speaking, count as male). But unless you are a brazen strumpet, you will never before have spent time alone in a man's company and you will need some schooling in the subject – remember, your duty and future contentment depend on inveigling them into offering a marriage proposal. You must be charming but slightly aloof; attentive but not worldly (innocence is everything in the mind of a prospective husband).

If you have ever wondered about the inner workings of a gentleman, including their strange practices and interests, read on.

CONVERSATION WITH A GENTLEMAN

Naturally, you must wait for a gentleman to strike up conversation with you, as propriety dictates you must be formally introduced before he can so much as glance at you, let alone speak to you or invite you to dance.

Being a witty conversationalist is encouraged, though do not be so cultivated that you pose a threat to his intellectual capacity (even though we all know who holds the superior rank on that front). You may mention some of your pursuits, including your proficiency in the pianoforte, needlework and flower-pressing. Do not mention reading, as this can be a dangerous pastime for a lady, for it has the potential to confuse one's thoughts. After a mere moment reflecting on your passions, you must fully immerse yourself in the interests of the gentleman for the duration of your *tête-à-tête*.

ACCEPTABLE TOPICS OF CONVERSATION: Any of his recent achievements, such as a horse race, fencing and hunting, then move on to town distractions versus rustic country pleasures, Oxford, and specifically japes at Oxford involving livestock.

DROP EUROPEAN TERMS INTO PARLANCE WHEN YOU CAN: It's charming and it will make you appear most cultured. For example, *ménage à trois* (which means the trials of managing your three lady's maids), *inflagrante delicto* (a very beautiful flame-coloured flower) and *cunnilingus* (a language enthusiast and keen polyglot). These expressions are sure to impress, showing off your natural aptitude for languages and interest in travel.

WHAT NOT TO DISCUSS: Card-game fallouts, gambling debts (gentlemen of ill repute do not pay their debts), Bloomsbury mistresses or any rumours you've heard about the gentleman's club (what happens at da club, stays at da club).

I barely need write this, as it should not need repeating, but as I mentioned earlier, you must never be alone with a gentleman; it is most improper and could prove ruinous for your prospects if this lapse is discovered.

HOW TO AVOID THE ADVANCES OF A BRUTE

You have followed the rules above and become so entrancing that every cad in town wants in. You see the Marquess of Twiddletormy making a beeline for you, sloppy eyes (they rotate independently of each other) on your buxom empire line, birch wine sloshing over his breeches. It simply won't do, so here's how to make an escape:

- Initiate a conversation with another gentleman and suddenly start laughing wildly at everything he says (even if he says nothing and is staring at you in confusion).
- If he cannot be avoided, reference your 'women's problems' while in conversation with him, or say the word 'discharge'.
- A timely swoon (see page 71 for a step-by-step guide) is an effective get-out for all sorts of hapless situations. But be sure to do it in the direction of a more suitable suitor.

BUSTING THOSE BALLS

Dearest debutantes, you cannot underestimate the significance of a ball; I implore you to prepare meticulously and do not stray from these rules of decorum.

NAIL THOSE DANCE MOVES

Nothing is more erotic to a gentleman than observing you side-step in two-four time during a Scotch reel. It is a sight that will entice even the most modest of types, turning them into lusty lotharios in an instant. And if they catch a view of your ankles, they'll be driven wild with desire.

So, getting one's freak on will be what captures the attention of suitors

and your moves will be one of your greatest assets.
Practise these dances with your governess with
unwavering commitment and your notable
accomplishments will not go unnoticed:

WALTZ: A flirty little number that will see you getting up
   close with your dashing beau and gliding elegantly
   around the ballroom. Avoid the garlic eel canapés
   before this entanglement.

COTILLION: Titillating and risqué. You will be frequently
   changing partners here, so this is a sensational
   opportunity to charm en masse.

QUADRILLE: An amusing frolic *à quatre* – you'll need
   your wits about you. Put a foot wrong and you could
   be face-planting into the loins of a bounder (sending all
   kinds of wrong signals).

Do not be too hasty to fill up your dance card of an
evening. Remember that saying yes to crusty old Lord
Snaresfiddle may mean you later have to say no to the
spicy Viscount Villesforce. And dancing with the same
gentleman more than once at any given ball is extremely
forward; you are basically betrothed.

HOW MANY BALLS SHOULD ONE ATTEND IN A SEASON?

A delicate balance to strike – too many and you may look desperate, too few and you risk insulting the Queen with your apathy.

And should one dance every dance? While the demanding nature of night-long dancing demonstrates your health and vitality and boasts your natural predisposition to bearing heirs, there can be strategic work carried out from the sidelines, too. Observe no fewer than two reels while quaffing an elderberry shrub, looking radiant and engaging in witty repartee with a stud of rank. '*The most perfect thing for you to do now is not to dance but leave them wanting more.*' True fact.

Always leave the party early; pace yourself, for the season is long – even the brightest stars may dim quickly.

WHO TO SET YOUR SIGHTS ON?

In the run-up to your first season, preparation is everything. See the Gentlemen Catalogue on page 157 for this season's most eligible bachelors.

Of course, a love match is a desirable outcome (provided, of course, the lineage of the coupling is not compromised). As Lady Bridgerton would attest, marrying one's dearest friend is favourable.

Who doesn't want romance, instant spark and that tingling feeling in your gusset when your betrothed fastens your loose cuff button? But let's be pragmatic: while love may be a pleasant diversion, the priority of the union is to secure the pedigree of the line, joining together grand families such as yours, rightfully preserving the aristocracy and keeping the rabble in their place.

Naturally, your father, uncle or brother will assume the role of matchmaker. While it's true that men hold much of the power in the marriage market – their preparation for a ball involves sauntering and champagne-swilling in contrast to your near asphyxiation as your maid stuffs you into your whale-bone corset – you do hold some influence as to who you wish to target. Discreetly, though – a woman showing conspicuous ambition is a vulgar trait indeed.

So, who will solicit your attention – a rakish marquess, a dapper duke or perhaps an eloquent earl?

KEEPING YOUR AMBITIOUS MAMA IN CHECK

Your beloved mama. Close confidante. Domineering fireball.

It's at least two decades since your dear mama's entrance into society and she's most enthralled for you to reach this milestone. But it's roused in her a somewhat frenzied, hysterical state of mind.

DOES MAMA ALWAYS KNOW BEST?

She'll be watching, most indiscreetly, wittering and tittering from the wings and later analysing your achievements (or admonishing any faux pas). She wants the best for you, of course she does, and she wants to see a good match made. She similarly needs to ensure you set a precedent for your younger siblings by marrying successfully. But while she means well, that's not to say she can't be rather vexing at times as she fiendishly tries to orchestrate the task at hand. So, how to control your tiger mama?

- Start small. A well-timed withering stare in the direction of an overbearing mama is sometimes all that's needed.

- Cranking it up a notch, if your mama remains all up in your bidness, ask her how one comes to be with child. She'll be out of there quicker than you can say Lord Wetherby's whiskers.
- And finally, if you have no choice but to go all out, trick her with a cunning ruse to get her off your petticoat tails and give you some breathing space (corset allowing …) to consider which debonair gent to accept. Form an attachment – purely superficial, of course – with a gentleman who shares a vested interest in seeming hooked up. Let society see you together – locked in a dancing embrace at a ball, licking ice-cream spoons in a café, promenading in the park – and marvel at your handsomeness. Have him send you (and your mama) some extravagant blooms from the most outrageously decadent florist in Mayfair. Perhaps this gent wishes to fool the masses on account of a deeply embedded Oedipus complex and strange unwillingness to sire an heir. Whatevs, just find someone trustworthy who will keep up with your caper and get that pesky mama off your cloak.

There you have it: your apprenticeship into flawless etiquette. But the hard work is just beginning – follow the next steps in this guide for your ultimate makeover (which, judging from your current do, is much needed).

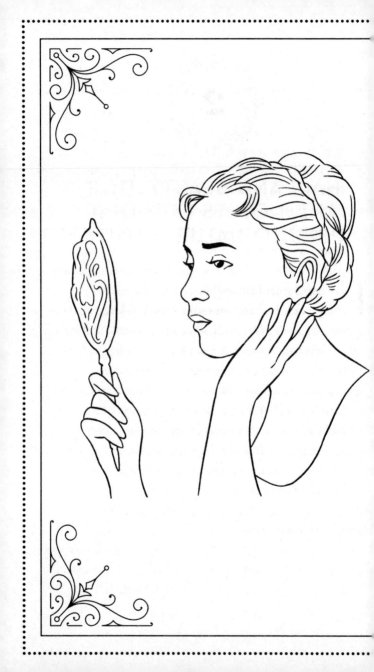

2

HAIR AND BEAUTY: DOS AND DON'TS FOR THAT PSEUDO-NATURAL LOOK

I have heard it said around the bridge table that having a nice face and agreeable hair is not an accomplishment. What toff – of course it is! Let's be in no doubt – your face and hot bod are your greatest assets in this, your opening season. Your studious dedication to the harpsichord and scholarly learnings of Latin will only take you so far. You must look sublime, radiant and ethereal in order to maximise your chances of successful husband hunting.

What's that you say, gentle reader? You look like the back end of your coachman's old nag? Fear not, because as with most aspects of a lady's life, one can fake it 'til one makes it.

MAXIMISING ONE'S VISAGE

Clear skin and a glowing complexion are not merely pleasing to the eyes of a gent, but will also prove that no smallpox or cholera have darkened the door of your household – always a nice bonus.

Your skin must be smooth and luminous, because any blemishes are a clear sign that you are ill-born. Note that it is unseemly for your face to weather, unless you are a field peasant. Perambulate with a parasol should the mercury reach 15°C or higher, and wear lace gloves unless you want to have the hands of a washerwoman.

A DRAWN COUNTENANCE

You've been on the sherry the night before at Lady Lanningbottom's ball for debutantes, partying hard until dawn, and after only forty winks in your bedchamber you're up again to welcome suitors in the morning room. You've no choice but to get up and put a brave face on it, although you look like a repulsive ogre.

Your mama is ringing the bell frantically, summoning

you to charm your callers – today could be the day of a proposal. The only thing for it is a mini facial – have your maid bring you the freshest mule urine she can find and apply it generously to the face and neck. Rinse with a tonic made from arsenic and you will be revived beyond recognition.

IT'S GLOW TIME!

Thank heavens, gone is the fashion of yesteryear for the heavily painted faces slathered in white powder (I blame the French for spreading such a fiendish fad). Unless you're a lady of the stage or, perish the thought, *even* worse than that, you will be a paragon of (pseudo) natural beauty. Let your radiance appear effortless and by the time your future groom realises what you actually look like *au natural*, it will be the morning after your wedding (and therefore too late for him to do anything about it).

EYES: A subtle smoky eye will be sure to catch the attention of a potential suitor. Simply apply some burnt cork to your lashes and brows (but beware of going to excess here – you're not in Soho).

CHEEKS: A crimson shine is vulgar, while the light tint of a youthful glow will bring luminosity. Your lady's maid can rustle up a vermilion rouge, but ensure it's applied sparingly lest you look like you are afflicted by typhoid fever.

LIPS: Apply a light pink pomade, drawing attention to your sensuous assets, and have callers form an orderly queue.

BEAUTY SPOT: Feel free to play around with the placement of this depending on the occasion and your mood (placed on your left cheekbone, it signals you are ready for diversion, but drawn on your right it denotes 'approach with caution' – do not get confused in the looking glass). Just be mindful of having it too near one's mouth if you are anticipating any discreet encounters in a night-time garden.

STRAY HAIRS: Tame the beast – if you are unfortunate enough to have inherited your father's whiskers, I implore you to have any rogue hairs extracted with force. Spare a thought for your potential suitors (who do not wish to be reminded of their great-uncle Octavius when they look at you).

STUBBLE RASH: If matters have got out of hand with a certain duke, you will be left with a tell-tale bristle rash as a calling card. The only remedy for this is applying liberally onto the affected area(s) the milk of a wet nurse (extracted from said wench within the previous hour) and it will be soothed before your next engagement.

EXPRESS YOURSELF

Perfecting that exquisite doe-eyed expression is particularly advantageous when enamouring a gentleman. Quite different to the pout, which is all about maintaining a level of imperiousness while still somehow looking hot.

Mastering a coy facade that is a touch morose is more challenging than you may imagine – appearing deep in thought without having Bitchy Resting Face takes skill. Be careful you do not furrow your brow too much here, as that is not appealing:

STEP 1: Make eye contact, then look away bashfully.

STEP 2: Return to meet his gaze and smile skittishly.

STEP 3: Allow him to kiss your hand as you titter politely.

STEP 4: What a performance! You are basically engaged now.

IS YOUR BOD BALLROOM-READY?

Exactly ninety-nine days before the start of the season, you must curtail your food intake by three-quarters. Your gown fittings will commence some weeks before the opening ball and if you don't begin reducing early enough, you'll be risking sow-in-a-dress territory. Remember, modistes get aggressive around this time of year on account of their pressing workload and they are known to bite ladies (of any rank) who possess surplus skin.

Take every meal in the drawing or dining room while standing up – not only will this keep you svelte, it will show you at your best angles for any suitor who may call.

BREAKFAST: A pewter egg cup half-filled (and no more!) with veal.

LUNCH: This is a no-go. If you feel peckish around this time, go to sleep.

DINNER: One-third of an artichoke may be consumed and a thimble of kidney.

SUPPER: Boiled water with spices.

Who said starvation had to be unappealing? You'll love these easy swaps each day:

PORTLY PRE-SEASON YOU	OPENING-BALL READY
• Mutton chops with liver	• A saucer of turnip shavings
• Pigeon pie	• Three peppercorns soaked in claret
• Calves' foot jelly	• Partridge carcass broth
• Marzipan syllabub	• A single nettle stewed in four quarts of sea water

For more delicious recipes that Cook can rustle up, turn to page 109.

Every astute lady knows that to complement a ration rebate, exercise must be endured. You must start doing everything expeditiously – marginal gains – whether it's bashing out an arpeggio on the pianoforte with veracity or catching up with one's correspondence using frantic penmanship. A side effect of starvation is hanger, so channel this rage into frenzied productivity.

PLAYING BRIDGE: A surprising way to banish the blubber – deal that deck like you mean it, lengthen your arms while flinging the cards down with agility and strength, and enjoy acquiring guns more powerful than the late Viscount Bridgerton's pistol.

PERAMBULATION: Leave the carriage at home and take at least one daily constitutional – Mayfair is the perfect spot for this; a place to see and be seen. An added benefit of walking is that it may be done in the company of a gentleman (provided there is a chaperone lingering not far behind). If you are feeling faint (which you will be if you are following my dietary advice), it is quite proper to take his arm. When you are at home, run swiftly up and down the servants' staircase while hoisting the heaviest volumes in your papa's library.

EMBROIDERY: A workout for those bingo wings: sew like you mean it. Thread the needle with dramatic purpose, lifting it up high in the air after each stich. Be careful, though, this can be a dangerous pursuit and this is the reason Lady Finnyhatton now wears an eye patch.

HORSE RIDING: Saunter through Hyde Park, trot through the rolling English hills, gallop to a duel. It will grant you the thigh gap of a Trojan warrior princess (which will also come in handy for the below).

ATHLETIC LOVEMAKING: Put your back into it, girl. Obviously, this is only an option IF you are married or have no prospects. For more tips on how to be a skilled lover, go to page 83.

HAIR TODAY, HAIR TOMORROW

One's hair has a story to tell and yours is no exception. Take heed of the advice here – what a shame it would be to have worked so hard getting all bootilicious only for your barnet to let you down.

It's crucial for a debutante such as yourself to play to your strengths – accentuate those foxy features and distract from any unbecoming characteristics. When it comes to hair, it must work with your face; they need to be the best of friends, one perfectly complementing the other. In order to do this, you must establish whether you possess, a) a lean visage, not dissimilar to that of your favourite hunting hound, or b) a face round and plump like one of Cook's skillets. Gaze into the looking glass and be honest with yourself – your hair happiness depends on it. If you answered a, congratulations, all of these dos will look comely, if b, commiserations, your work is cut out for you.

THE UP-DO: A demure, prim arrangement, perfectly suitable for those times that call for modesty – you might wear this to a private audience with your regent. Your hair will be lifted off the neck and tied into pretty wraps and plaits, studded with the most delicate diamond flowers. This will allow your whole face to be clearly on view, so ensure there are no love nuzzles on your neck. A substantial up-do can also double as a handbag, where there will easily be room to store essentials and snacks.

THE HALF-UP, HALF-DOWN: You will need perfect curls to frame your face, with sections of your hair swept up into twists and secured with jewels to match your ensemble. A flirty

little arrangement, this
says you're traditional
but up for breaking the
rules on occasion – a
spirit that is irresistible
to a gentleman.

FRINGE: A short fringe
with a centre parting –
admittedly not the
easiest look to pull off. If
you are rounder of face,
steer clear, otherwise you
will look more like a
medieval monk.

RINGLETS AND CURLS: If
your maid is still styling
your hair in this childish
manner, release her from
your services at once.
She clearly despises you
and wants you to
become an old maid.

This is a most juvenile look, one that will win you no
attention among suitors.

As a side note, when you really wish to make an entrance, consider adding a bird cage or some other wildlife to your hair to liven things up a tad.

As a married lady, you will enjoy some 'spirited' activities with your new husband (see Chapter 6 – though you are only permitted to read this chapter once he's put a ring on it). These dalliances will affect your previously sleek locks and now you'll look like you've been dragged through a hedge. Do not fret. Your servants will know what to do and will discipline your unruly mane.

REVENGE HAIR

This is where you pull out the big guns – you know, for those times when the gentleman you were courting, who seemed to be into you, suddenly stops inviting you out for intimate spoon-licking sessions. The circlet of jewels and flowers is reserved for such occasions – perfectly flowing hair and a tiara of dazzling stones and feathers. With hair this good, you really won't need to settle for a duke when a prince comes a-calling.

Now, dearest reader, take all the wisdom you have gathered here and combine it with the sartorial rules laid out in the next chapter, and what an enticing parcel you will be. Swish!

3

REGENCY REGALIA: DRESS TO IMPRESS (A DUKE, PRINCE OR VISCOUNT)

As a young lady, your wardrobe speaks volumes about you and your status in high society. You will be judged not just on what you wear but how you wear it. It's imperative you keep up with the latest fashions, remaining an icon and source of inspiration for fellow debutantes, who will aspire to be as dapper as you.

Externally you will look as pleasing as a Greek goddess, though hiding beneath the layers of luxurious silks and satins lies a different story. Yes, that's correct, the magic behind your silhouette is of course your best friend/greatest foe: the corset. You must adhere to varying levels of restriction to match the occasion – barely breathing for balls, short gasps to promenade and loosened only slightly further for bed. If your torso is not lacerated with cuts and bruising, your undergarments are simply not tight enough and you need to be wrung with brute force. Fret not – once you have ensnared your gentleman into marriage, the corset strings can be loosened and you can let yourself go.

CURATING YOUR CAPSULE WARDROBE

It can be vexing to decipher what to wear each day, such is the diversity of your wardrobe, but therein lies the problem: too much choice. Overloading your delicate brain with more trivial decision-making so early in the day can distract you from the essential task in hand: finding a suitable husband. The solution? You must cultivate a collection that works, whether you are in the town or country. For example:

TEA-DRINKING IN THE DRAWING ROOM: A gown (empire line).

A BALL: A gown (empire line). Rev it up with a tiara.

HORSE RIDING: A gown (empire line) and a velvet cloak (if haste is your aim, cloaks are well known for making your horse gallop faster).

PICKING LAVENDER IN THE GARDEN: A gown (empire line).

CULTURAL EVENTS SUCH AS THE THEATRE, OPERA AND EXHIBITIONS: A gown (empire line), jazzed up with a semi-opaque shoulder wrap.

YOUR WEDDING: A gown (empire line), accessorised with a veil.

PIG CONTEST: A gown (empire line) with long sleeves.

Tea drinking in
the ballroom

A ball

Horse riding

Picking lavender
in the garden

Cultural events such as the theatre, opera and exhibitions

Your wedding

Pig contest

BOSOM BUDDIES

While decorum dictates that your gown must cover you all the way down to your satin slippers (you may show a little ankle on your wedding night), your rack must be almost fully exposed at all times.

Be mindful, though, that a heaving bosom says it all; indeed, it is as expressive as your face – even more so perhaps. Joy, confusion, lost virtue – your bosom can betray your every emotion, and therefore you must keep it in check. This may be used to your advantage when you wish to send coded cleavage messages to potential admirers.

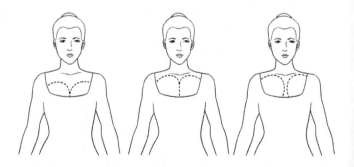

The high-tops   The push 'n' lift   The slide and glide

THE HIGH-TOPS: Your cleavage should ideally be so high that you can almost rest your chin on it (you will need more help achieving this as the years go on). Secret meaning: Come hither, my lord.

THE PUSH 'N' LIFT: You'll have to rearrange your internal organs for this one. Your lady's maid must be as strong as an ox to ensure ultimate tension. Do not hire puny help for this reason. Secret meaning: Don't dally with my affections, I mean business.

THE SLIDE AND GLIDE: There should be a slight gap between each bosom here, but they should be so elevated that the clavicle will get in their way. Secret meaning: I'm a lady of complicated depths. Learn my inner workings and treat me as your equal so that we may enter a partnership built not just on love, but admiration and mutual respect.

WHO WORE IT BEST?

You must never wear the same gown twice or it will look like your family has entered financial ruin. Banish any talk of repurposing fabrics. It simply won't do.

Be cautious about adopting lurid, tawdry colours (favoured by a certain family that possesses socially mobile aspirations, with three daughters currently all out in society at once – most improper), as you'll be catching the eye for all the wrong reasons. If it resembles the colour of an English hard cheese, refrain. Instead opt for subtle hues, virginal white, tasteful pastels and muted tones that will accentuate your natural beauty.

Things you can hide under a shawl:

- A burgeoning bulge (most shameful – let us hope gestational arithmetic is not the strong point of the gentleman you entrap into marriage).
- Your most treasured copy of *Flawless, My Dear*.
- Your notebook and quill, for documenting the scandal of the day.

AUTUMN/WINTER 1813 ACCESSORY TRENDS

It's not all about the dress, dear reader. How you accessorise can lift you victorious from a sartorial slump and propel you into the fashion-forward maven you are.

HARNESS THAT HEADWEAR

The I've-nothing-to-wear anxiety can be nipped in the bud by some clever headwear.

MAKING YOUR BONNET WORK FOR YOU: A fine bonnet denotes one's Ton status, and provided one keeps a wide brim, it will show the face in a most favourable manner – important when taking a daily saunter. Ladies who place their bonnets at a jaunty angle may think they appear jolly and youthful, but they actually look mentally imbalanced. If you wish to make your bonnet more convivial, you are permitted to add a fine silk ribbon (one in a shade that will complement your empire-line gown).

PLUMAGE: Just as a gentleman struts like a peacock, so too can you enjoy some aviary inspiration. A delicate feather subtly protruding from your 'do' hints at your ruling-class heritage, but also shows a softer side in your respect for the natural world. Tread carefully, though – too many feathers or ones in garish hues will have you looking like a show girl on a circus pony (but not in a good way).

WIGGING OUT: I am often asked for my considered opinion on such aesthetic matters. Among the most common is, 'Dearest Wibberfluffle, can I rock a wig?' You have seen some spectacular ladies in high society bring height and sophistication to their person, and you want a piece of that pie. I'm afraid it's highly unlikely you can get away with such a bold visual. We cannot all be blessed with the natural style of Queen Charlotte and her ability to sport a wig as big as the newly built east wing of Buckingham Palace. Balancing a crown atop a wig is a tall order. Literally. Purple, white, neon, with diamonds, feathers and butterflies – more is more when it comes to our beloved Regent. But it is not the look for an aspiring debutante.

GODDESS GLOVES

Needless to say, these are a must-have and if you dare to leave your residence without them, you will appear very low-bred.

How they are worn can reveal a lot about your current state of mind:

- *Long, silk, over-the-elbow gloves:* You need a confidence boost.
- *Low, sheer, wrist-length gloves:* You are emboldened and feeling daring.
- *Leather gloves:* Optimism is in the air and you're feeling frisky – you take your mare out for a side-saddle trot around Hyde Park.
- *Furry muff:* Show off your muff and flaunt it with pride whenever you enjoy a turn about Mayfair.

Take care of your muff and your muff will take care of you.

When you wed, your groom will remove your gloves from your hands at the altar, finger by finger, in such a seductive way that you may pass out with lust – how awkward that your family are watching. He will also relish doing this at the dining table in front of embarrassed servants. Just go with it – it's a strange pleasure he enjoys, but then gentlemen have many unusual pastimes.

FANNYING AROUND

Do not be afraid to use your accessories as props in your quest to find a husband. Look no further than the fan – the big daddy of accessories – as the ultimate prop for wooing.

FIVE WAYS WITH A FAN

1. Fan yourself seductively, whatever the weather, slowly and delicately, with your fan positioned in front of your impressive bosom.
2. 'Drop' your fan coquettishly at the feet of a handsome prince and he will be beholden to you. Let him pick it up and as he slowly stands he will take in the view of you from toes to nose, appreciating a fine specimen in

all your glory. Be sure there is a significant crowd watching and marvelling.

3. Flirt wildly with a gentleman and draw your fan up to hide your blushes while remaining locked in eye contact. A most charming affectation.

4. Wave your fan gracefully, drawing attention to your unworked hands and fingers.

5. If someone displeases you, snap your fan shut for the ultimate diss.

JEWELS

To achieve 'diamond of the season' status, your jewellery must work hard for you. A lady who is not appropriately bejewelled is effectively nude and can expect to be libelled by Lady Whistledown herself, almost as if she had arrived at the Royal Academy clad only in her undergarments. Jewellery not only complements a lady's exquisiteness, adding vivacity and polish; it also displays the wealth of one's family and offers a reminder of the handsome dowry that will accompany you into your marriage contract. This writer has heard vicious rumours that 'ladies' among the middle-class ranks have audaciously started to don jewels (no doubt semi-precious rather than precious stones), so it has never been more imperative for an astute lady to assert her position through the jewels she wears. Once married these will become even more exuberant. More is more, dear debutante, and now is the time to radiate opulence – just be sure never to go larger than the Queen. Upstaging her would be treasonous.

DAZZLING JEWELS THAT WILL LIGHT UP ANY BALLROOM

Earrings, necklace, bracelets, tiara, brooches and bling rings – they must all work in harmony rather than fight against each other.

GEM-STONED CHOKERS: These are not for everyone – if you are remotely jowly, stay far, far away as you do not possess the delicate elegance to sport one. If you are wider than a chess board, do not even stand beside a lady wearing a choker.

DIAMONDS: Representing purity and chastity, there will be more of these precious stones coming to a ring finger near you, should you follow the instructions in this guide.

PEARLS: A classic statement of tradition and elegance.

EMERALDS: Worn to enhance breeding capabilities, these should be staples of your honeymoon accessories.

FLAUNT THAT NAPE

Sparkling gems will not only catch the flickering lights of candelabras, they will also draw attention to the most elegant parts of a lady's physique: the nape. Just imagine a handsome Prussian prince delicately placing a diamond necklace around your neck, gently lowering it to rest on your collarbone as you feel his breath (while you daydream about another bloke). In the end, a wasted gift from his point of view, but very fetch nonetheless.

So, my dear reader, you are equipped with all you need to look ravishing (yet innocent), and you are ready to take the next foray into your debutante finishing school by learning all you need to know about the murky world of power and morality.

4

HONOUR, MORALS
(WHEN TO HAVE THEM)
AND POWER

This author is here to inform you that all is not as it may seem in the Ton. There are intricate structures of honour and power, and a code of ethics to follow, if you wish to preside in society as a significant lady. You will need to demonstrate propriety and decorum all the time, should you wish to retain properness and influence (except when you throw it all out of the window to ensnare a gentleman by whatever means are available to you). It is also prudent to recognise when the gentlemen hold the power and when it lies with you (which, fortunately, is more often than you may imagine).

HONOUR

As a young lady, your virtue is one of your prime assets (up there with your superior rack) and of the utmost importance. As I have mentioned once or twice, you shall remain chaste and innocent until your wedding – because, as you know well, so much as a salacious glance between you and the opposite sex would cast you out from high society. And quite rightly. But what should one do if one finds their honour in peril? My dear reader, one's honour is everything and must be protected.

In the next chapter, I'll instruct on how a timely uppercut can put in his place any swine who tries to take liberties with one's virtue. And similarly, how feigning a romantic attachment with a high-society hottie can be a short-term means to protecting one's honour from ne'er-do-wells who attempt to interfere with it. But what is a lady to do when she is in the thick of a reputation-smear campaign that attempts to discredit her? Read these rules and do not waver from them.

RULE NUMBER 1: Deny everything. As you represent competition to other ladies on the marriage market, they will relish any opportunity to defame your good name, trolling you all over the Ton with delight. Your social frenemy may have spotted you canoodling, but it's your word against hers. Haters gonna hate. Put her in her place with a clapback (that contains a hint of a threat). One does what one needs to do to win.

RULE NUMBER 2: Keep your eye on the prize. You fancy him. He's got childhood PTSD. Stick with it and don't relent until you've dragged him down the aisle (kicking and screaming is fine, if necessary).

RULE NUMBER 3: Get a ring on it. If you've been up to no good, act quickly (see page 79 for how to expedite a marriage licence).

Do bear in mind that the rules are very different for gentlemen, who prefer to settle matters of honour over a duel. Allow me to explain this custom.

THE DUEL

A duel is a rite of passage for a gentleman and the most straightforward and reasonable way of reconciling a disagreement and protecting honour. No matter is too large or too trivial to be settled by a duel. Offended a young lady's honour? Get those pistols out. Questioned

the length of a
gentleman's sideburns?
Lock and load. The fact
that it's illegal is no
matter for a discerning
gentleman. It's a question
of honour.

A gent must be sure
to wrap up any loose
ends before duelling. Just
in case. Mistresses need
to be provided for
should the worst happen,
and a final pity shag will
be expected; pocket
watches handed over.

HOW TO ACE A DUEL

So, what are the steps a gentleman must take before a duel
and how might they plan for one?

1. It is essential a gentleman stays up imbibing the whole
   night before a duel, slurping with intent a glass of
   brandy at all times (never letting it fall below two
   fingers' worth). This keeps the mind sharp and the
   trigger finger poised for action come dawn.

2. Select a location for the duel – somewhere leafy and pretty and horsey.
3. Choose a 'second' carefully – the gentleman needs someone loyal at their side, someone who has no vested interest in seeing them die or absconding to the Continent (where they would live a rakish existence, lying low on the fringes of European society).
4. Count your steps and fire. Ideally both men will have terrible shots and no harm will come to either (but not so bad that a bystanding horse gets the brunt of it).
5. But the most compelling method of acing a duel is simply to plan and discuss it at great length, but then avoid actually having it. This needs to be orchestrated in a way where neither party loses face.

MORALS

Lies, deception, extortion – they have all been in abundance during this exciting season. But how important are morals? Choose carefully, as they are often overrated. I have included below some of the questions (redacted to preserve the anonymity of those asking) that readers have recently written to me in the 'Ask Wibberfluffle' column of my weekly periodical (I am viewed as quite the sage in

the Ton). Allow my wisdom to guide your moral compass in those times when you're unsure of the most appropriate course of action.

FIDELITY

Dear Duchess Wibberfluffle,
My fiancé seems to be playing the field – does that give me licence to do the same?
> Yours,
> Confused but up for it, Knightsbridge

While as a young lady you should remain unblemished, for a young gent (or even an older, married one) about the Ton, it is an imperative to have a mistress. She should be lower-born (but not a pot washer) as the social gap between positions in society will debase morals further, allowing the gentleman to feel even more superior (a sense of superiority, even when unmerited, is a great turn-on for a gentleman).

The gent is permitted to string her along endlessly (and finally ghost her), but should she have the audacity to enjoy other friends-with-benefits relationships, he is fully entitled to lose it and storm around London in a rageful frenzy.

I'm afraid you will not be permitted to enjoy the same privileges as a single lady; but, once you are firmly installed as the lady of the manor, you may find you and your philandering husband can come to some arrangement regarding extra-marital amusements.

BETRAYAL

Dear Duchess Wibberfluffle,

As a newly married lady, I crave to be blessed with an infant. Alas, my husband does not. Would it be terribly wrong to take advantage of him during his 'crescendo'?

Yours,

Childless and unhappy, Grosvenor Square

Previously unbeknownst to you, he has made his mind up never to be a father – and has hidden the true reason from you. The scoundrel. And what a dilemma you now face (this author does enjoy a spot of jeopardy). Look, no one said adulting was going to be easy; you've been royally mugged off, but is angry betrayal sex really the answer? Conspiring to force him to deposit his seed into the one location the servants will not have to clean up cannot be condoned.

FRAUD

Dear Duchess Wibberfluffle,
My husband has plunged us into financial ruin (I
even had to re-wear a gown to a ball) – how shall we
escape it?
Yours,
Poverty-stricken, Mayfair

As we know, gentlemen need to fill up the days and nights
with merriment while we sew and practise the harp. One
such pleasure is gambling, which they often combine with
another diversion: sport (in this case the 'sport' is watching
men attack each other). But what can a fellow do when he
is down on his luck? There is only one solution: fix a
boxing match. This will allow a crooked gentleman to
settle his arrears across the Ton while the athlete in
question may put food on the table for his many urchin
children. A low blow, but sometimes one can't afford
morals and fraud is the answer. Note that there are no
victors here. Apart from the ones who benefit financially.

DERELICTION OF DUTY

Dear Duchess Wibberfluffle,
Try not to be shocked – I am an unmarried lady
with child and the father of this infant is not
responding to my letters requiring him to
acknowledge paternity and wed me. What shall I
do?
　Yours,
　Sad, alone and rotund, Eaton Square

So, you've met a dashing officer – in church of all places
(candles, incense, ambient lighting: you can see how it's
Regency England's hottest hook-up destination) – and one
thing has led to another. It isn't long before your courses
have failed to arrive. Your plucky musketeer is now on the
Continent fighting for king and country and you need to
tell him the news so that he can take leave to wed you. But
how does one chase down a soldier who has left you with
a misbegotten child? Connections are important here.
Infiltrate a MLG (see page 98 for more on the benefits of a
married ladies' group) and you may be helped in locating
his battlefield.

　Holding a gentleman to account is right and proper as
they must face up to their moral responsibility. As Lady
Featherington explains, a gentleman may be quick to make

declarations of affection, but when the fruits of his loins are brought to his attention, he tends to bounce right out of there.

If all else fails, trick a wide-eyed gent into marrying you. You won't be winning any morality awards here, but needs must. Do you want to live in a Covent Garden slum with your illegitimate child after you have been shunned from polite society? Let not a gentleman shame you for your actions. Stand proud(ish), for you have been forced into this by the deeds of another reckless man and left with little choice (not that this writer should ever have conducted herself so shamefully).

POWER

It may seem like the gentlemen of the Ton have all the power, call all the shots, but, reader, we know it's a very different story. It's we ladies of society who get sh*t done. Behind every man is a tigress pulling the strings to their advantage. Whether taking matters into one's own hands by driving away barbaric suitors (see page 13) or announcing one's own engagement to the groom (page 78), our poise and pragmatism bolster society. Let us be discreet about this power, though, as we do not wish the men to know who truly wears the breeches.

Here are some everyday ways by which a lady may exercise influence.

WISTERIA HYSTERIA

Do not underestimate the subtle power of foliage – the height of your wisteria shows the extent of your superiority. Have your town residence clad in this opulent lilac vine and ensure at least six gardeners are responsible for its maturation. Similarly, the climbing prowess of your ivy will leave no one in any doubt as to who's boss. It is prudent to remember that plants are empathetic beings that channel our emotions, so take note that your wisteria will be reflecting your family's good fortune to the Ton. Any cracks and your wisteria will know about it and, in turn, display it.

Should it be more prolific than the Queen's? Sedition to even consider it.

HOW TO DRIVE A GENTLEMAN WILD WITH JEALOUSY

There are many ways in which to do this, but one of the most effective is at the aforementioned boxing exhibition (whether you believe this sport to be barbarous is no matter). A strange location, you might assume, and your mama would admonish you that it's no place for a lady, but is that truly the case? On closer inspection, it is the ideal venue: buff, topless athletes and a ridiculously favourable gentleman-to-lady ratio will mean you stand out from the crowd. Whether you're a would-be duchess in the company of a prince (doing your bit for international relations) or an opera singer in attendance with a moustachioed cad but making eyes at a viscount, you will be noticed.

DOS AND DON'TS OF EMINENT-LADY LIFE

Should your marriage sustain or elevate you to being a lady of very high nobility (like myself), you will naturally gain more power and influence. Your primary role will be to support your husband as he manages the estate. The life of a gentleman may appear to be a merry-go-round of relaxing in the gentlemen's lounge and enjoying unusual sex positions with good-time gals, but there is also serious work to attend to and a gentleman must not become distracted from important business matters. There is much to be done on an estate: adjudicating livestock contests, pretending to care about wheat yields and keeping an eye on wayward stewards who triple land rents – and all while dining at very long tables. All of this is most taxing for a gentleman and your helping hand will be required.

As a duchess myself, I take great pleasure and expertise in offering my pearls of wisdom to the next generation of young ladies with pedigree. Should you find yourself making such an esteemed match, it is imperative you follow these guidelines:

- *Don't hassle the help:* Stay on your housekeeper's good side. Remember, she knows things about you (and your proclivities).
- *Pull rank:* It's not that you enjoy reminding plebs of your superior status, but you hold a commanding position among the Ton. Wear your bosom as high as you are in the instep.
- *Gossip:* Remember, one of our greatest gifts as ladies is our power of communication (and by that, I mean spreading scandal, where appropriate, for the greater

good, such as freeing a debutante from the clutches of a beastly engagement).

- *Animal matters:* Never call a tie at a pig contest (or indeed any livestock competitions). It creates bad feeling among the peasants and your head could be on a spike before you know it. If possible, stay out of all matters regarding animal husbandry.

- *The picture of married bliss:* Have your portrait painted as a couple, appointing a spirited artist of the day who is a fellow of the Royal Academy. Look imperious and sullen, but hot, then display this painting at the first extravagant ball you host (make sure it rains) as a married lady.

Ladies, you now know the truth of our complicated moral structure. What a tangled web we weave! Use all you have learned here to navigate your way into courtship and find the perfect match (and maybe even a love one at that).

5

LOVE AND COURTSHIP: YOUR HUSBAND-HUNTING COMPENDIUM

Dear reader, it's time to get down to business. Navigating the marriage market and finding true love (or, failing that, a match that does not bring shame) is why you are reading this guide, is it not? And while it is certainly optimal to pull during the first season, remember that high standards must be adhered to and a quick, ill-matched union may be a long source of regret.

This will be a time of first dalliances – you're fresh as a filly, raring to go and have thus far followed my advice to stay chaste. Continue to tread carefully, dear debutante. A false step could prove ruinous. But what if even your very best efforts are no match for a bounder who'll attempt to lure young you into their web of iniquity, having a fumble, or even worse?! Defiling your innocence and besmirching your honour – these men are rakes through and through. Admittedly, though, they are sometimes very charming and hard to resist, so heed my counsel to circumvent compromising situations.

In this chapter, I will hold your hand as you find your way through the perils of being a lady in want of a gentleman – whether it's a long courtship or a race to the altar.

TYPES OF HUSBAND

It is first pertinent to outline the key attributes of a gentleman. It's widely documented that there are five types of male – and five alone. Here is your guide to establishing the right fit for you (take counsel: several of these are duds – you must be able to spot these a country mile away and relish in the JOMO).

THE BROODER: He's down-to-earth (as gentlemen of rank go – sometimes he even has a beer rather than a brandy) and can pull off a spot of eye liner. But he's also troubled and, on top of it all, falls in love with the most unsuitable women – those with a 'paid occupation' (can you imagine?). Is it any wonder that rakes of this sort find it hard to settle down? Approach with caution – this suitor will guarantee an emotional rollercoaster.

THE DREAMER: Louche and affable, he seems uncomplicated, seeking trysts without any of the responsibility (and why not?), but don't be fooled – he still has many wild oats to sow and is far from ready to be marriage material. Don't waste your time on this one – he'll still be doing the rounds on what would be your fifth London season (when you'll be long settled, fourth infant in).

THE DANDY: Lads, lads, lads. A bit of a wildcard, he's been commitment-phobic up until now – that is, until he meets you. After a tough start in life, with no strong male role model to look up to, is it any wonder this rogue struggles to carve out a path for himself? Underneath it all, he's as soft as the goose-down in one of the Clyvedon Castle pillows; he feels all the feels – can you be the one who will penetrate that severe (but hot) exterior?

THE SCOUNDREL: He'll ravish you pre-engagement, then squander your recently attained dowry playing cards and chasing tail at Raffles. Stay away from this one. Swine.

THE SLEAZY, GROSS OLD GUY: Hairy chops, drooling and wandering hands – something's gone wrong here. Dare I ask what you did to end up with this match? The only saving grace is his advancing years – hopefully you won't have to wait long before he keels over and you can live your best life as a sexy widow.

OTHER IMPORTANT TRAITS TO SEEK:

- Sideburns: girth is as important as volume in this instance. The more the merrier. However, do not discount a gentleman on the basis of a shy sideburn, as his may have potential to be growers rather than showers.
- How many shirt ruffles is too many? Trick question, dear debutante, for there is no such thing.
- Can he hold his drink? What you're looking for is someone who enjoys a claret or two but knows when it's time to stumble into his carriage home.
- See how he spins. That's right. Just as a discerning gentleman will observe a lady's dance moves, so too will you judge a gentleman on how well he gets his groove on.

Now that you know how to identify these creatures, you have the tools at your disposal to send them come-hither vibes or avoid them like the new cholera epidemic.

PERFECTING THE ART OF THE SWOON

Keep a few tricks up the sleeve of your gown to entice suitors. Remember that nothing will make a man fall in love faster than competition – the challenge is to be a determined flirt while making it clear you are an untouchable virgin. Revisit Chapter 1 for a recap on feigning an attachment.

An opportune swoon, though somewhat ridiculous, can bring you the attentions of an eligible gentleman. It's particularly effective if the gent in question is a sap. You must follow this strict protocol, though:

- Look radiant. You must plan your swoon ahead of time; pre-meditation will allow you to pull out all the stops on your beauty regime (refer to Chapter 2 for more). Ensure one's nostrils are clear (no bats in the cave) and that you are smelling especially fragrant. Your bosom must be extra voluminous.
- Don't eat for at least four days in the run-up to the swoon. If you are so heavy that your intended cannot catch you, the swoon will backfire.
- When the time is right, lift your arm and place the back of your hand to your forehead. Grip the arm of your gentleman and delicately fall like a wilting flower.
- Let him fan you while marvelling at your fragile feminine disposition.

With all of the amazing advice you have gleaned in my guide thus far, it's likely you'll have gentlemen falling over their breeches to impress you. Not all of these fellows will be suitable, though, and you will have to bat their advances away, sometimes with force (for an in-depth tutorial, see 'How to refuse his hand', page 77).

MAKING YOUR MATCH

As we explored in Chapter 1, the slight sting in the tail of this marriage business is that much of the transaction will be orchestrated by one of the men in your life. With a bit of luck, you will have a papa who is discerning, calm and woke AF. He will cherry-pick a handful of the season's most eligible stallions and present them to you for your choice. He will not push you into a union you are not comfortable with, or present you with anyone odious/over the age of twenty-seven (elderly).

Alas, we ladies are not always this fortunate and sometimes other gentlemen – some of them paragons of dishonour themselves – are responsible for our wedded bliss (or horror show).

When he's not in compromising positions with his impressively flexible lover in the dressing room of the opera house, he's threatening duels or having a punch-up. That's right, your love life has been entrusted to your older brother (his many personal woes notwithstanding), who'll be attempting to secure your betrothal with all the subtlety of a rigged boxing match.

He's weirdly protective over you, yet seems ready to marry you off to any old bidder. The man he believes ticks all the boxes as a potential husband is unlikely to tick the most important box: your box. The one between your legs. If you're unsure what this means, please consult Chapter 6.

There's no doubt you'll have your work cut out for you here – managing the expectations of your clueless brother plus rejecting unwanted proposals left, right and centre.

FORGET YOUR FRIENDS

Your most dear gal pals. You've been frolicking together since you were in leading strings, playing in each other's nurseries, consoling one another when one's governess was too strict, and attempting to translate the confusing conversations of grown-ups. Inseparable. You'd do anything for each other – your friendship is the great love of your life. Or so you thought. Wrong! There are no friends when you are on the marriage market – only rivals. The marriage market creates opponents among young ladies. It's no time for loyalty. Get those knives out.

HE'S JUST NOT THAT INTO YOU

So, for the last decade you've been secretly in love with your BFF's older brother. Sure, he's a bit of a hunk, has a GSOH, can belt out a tune around the pianoforte and is quite the mover on the ballroom floor. He loves the company of ladies while having a deep respect for their virtue. You've always been able to talk freely with each other and you even hate the same people (surely the most important feature of a friendship), but still waters run deep with this guy. You feel a spark, but you're not quite picking up the same signals from him. Suddenly, there's a new sheriff in town and he's speaking rashly about proposals and gifts of tomatoes. There's no easy way to say this – you've been friend-zoned. Of course, you are a sophisticated lady, now out in society, but he still sees you as the girl next door, the slightly geeky friend of his sister. Fortunately, it didn't work out with the interloping harlot, but now he's heartbroken. And instead of proposing to you, he's about to embark on his tour, starting in the Mediterranean of all places.

A real blow, it must be said. Stay strong. Focus on your hobbies for now (walking up and down the stairs with a book on your head) and time will tell if he's worth waiting for.

DEAR DOWRY

The transactional aspect of your nuptials will be left in the hands of the patriarchy, where one gentleman must take on the duty of your wellbeing from another. Calculating one's dowry (anything less than five figures is pitiful, for sure) very much depends on whether one's father has squandered it all in gambling. This presents a challenge unless you can find a gentleman as enlightened as the Duke, who is insulted at the mere thought of being paid to marry and refuses to accept the dowry. And you know it is true love when he doesn't bat an eyelid on receipt of the bill his bride has racked up at the modiste.

Other aspects that affect one's dowry are one's accomplishments. Your embroidery and musical skills count for much here (no gentleman wishes to spend a lifetime suffering the racket of your pianoforte mishaps) – on the flip side, if you do not boast an ear for a melody and treat your instruments like you loathe them, your father will be extra keen to sell you off.

If all else fails, tell your suitor that all those pristine, recently published, first-edition Jane Austens you have stashed upstairs will be worth at least a few shillings one day.

Turn to page 166 to appraise your dowry's value.

HOW TO REFUSE HIS HAND

You've been working steadily all season towards securing a proposal. You've barely eaten in weeks and you've fake-smiled so much you are beginning to resemble a quokka – then lo and behold, an offer of marriage does come your way! But it's from Mayfair's most notorious ne'er-do-well. A villain through and through. So how do you reject his advances like you mean it?

PLANT A FACER!: Never underestimate the importance of a good right hook. It's unlikely you will find anyone to teach you this, but if you can find a prince to take you along to a bare-knuckle boxing match you will certainly be able to pick up some tips. It will come in very handy should you find yourself entrapped by a creep in a secluded garden (but make sure no one spots you or you will be ruined. Please see Chapter 1). Sorry, not sorry.

PUBLISH A SCANDAL ABOUT HIM: Your greatest weapon here is your lady's maid – charge her with infiltrating his household servants and uncovering something salacious about him. Then spread this all over the Ton and within hours watch the story unfold in print on the pages of Lady Whistledown's gazette. Watch in glee as the boorish brute flees before the day is out.

TURNING DOWN A PRINCE: A bold move, it must be said. You've enchanted the top dog, flirted outrageously with him, accepted his diamonds and – boom! – you're outta there. A trifle harsh, but the trick here is to go along with it until the eleventh hour and then, just before he pops the question, nip into the garden to romp with another chap. He'll get the message loud and clear.

SAY YES TO THE DRESS

It has happened. You've had a beautiful, romantic proposal from a gent who makes you as giddy as one of the Queen's Pomeranians. He's settled the financial side of things with your father/brother/uncle/random man on the street and has got down on one knee in a rose-filled garden and promises you he'll dedicate his life to making you happy. He's loaded and has a title to boot. Or alternatively, you're at a duel and he refuses to marry you, but you just go ahead and announce your engagement

anyway. Potato, pot-ato, one way or the other, you're betrothed.

What happens now? Here are your options:

GET THOSE BANNS READ: Time is of the essence here, especially if you've been up to no good (a month is far too long to the keep gossip-mongers at bay and you'll also be too frisky to wait). If you've been really saucy, seek a special dispensation from the Archbishop of Canterbury to expedite the marriage licence, or, failing that, plead your case to your monarch (royalty love a bit of filth and are often sympathetic).

BRAGGING RIGHTS: Promenade in public and demonstrate your superiority as a nearly married lady to all those pathetic single gals still slogging it through the season.

PREPARE THE TROUSSEAU (your maid will sort this – her wedding to-do list should be interminable; yours will be non-existent): Your trousseau will contain intimate items (not for you, but for the enjoyment of your fiancé), including:

- Five nightdresses (any fewer and you'll appear provincial).
- Three pantaloons: these should fall between the knee and ankle (a most arousing item for a gentleman).
- Four petticoats: worn underneath your gowns through the cold winter months. Essentially these are man-repellents, so they may come in useful once the honeymoon period is over.

GRETNA GREEN: YOUR GUIDE TO ELOPEMENT

Granted, this isn't the fairy-tale ceremony you've been dreaming about – you'd been envisioning a stately-manor-in-the-home-counties vibe rather than a destination wedding – but sometimes needs must. Gretna is your last resort for propriety – the go-to place to tie the knot if you've been devious.

Organise a carriage to the border, travelling in the dead of night. Tell no one. There will be much talk on your return, but this will be replaced by different gossip when your bastard offspring arrives six months later.

Well, dearest reader, you have sealed the deal, got spliced, plighted your troth. I would like to say my work here is done, but, fair bride, your education is only just beginning, for there is much to impart on the coming pages. But be warned, you are absolutely forbidden to read on unless you are a married lady.

6

LOVEMAKING LAID BARE: A GUIDE FOR INNOCENTS

How a lady comes to be with child may be the question on your lips. But on this an unmarried lady should receive no instruction. For, as we all know, a look of utter confusion and disgust is what every man expects to encounter on his wedding night – the proof that his bride is chaste. But for the purpose of selling books, this author will deign to share just enough knowledge to whet the appetite.

As a debutante, when trying to ascertain the meaning of sex it's important to ask everyone you know. Gathering the opinions from all you encounter on the subject can help you to sleuth the true meaning, slotting the pieces of this most befuddling jigsaw together. So, by all means, burst into the drawing room and demand answers from your mama, siblings and anyone else who may be hanging around sipping lapsang souchong. Investigate the subject with your BFF, going round in circles until you're even more mystified than when you started. As a married lady, TBH, you'll probably get more sense out of your lady's maid on the subject (she's been around the block). She's less prudish than your mama and she'll have to tell it to you straight because you are her mistress.

Don't wonder too much why the men of Mayfair all seem to know what it's about. They've been taking their sticks out for years since being initiated at Raffles.

SEX ED FROM YOUR MAMA

Well, this is awkward. Over the course of your wedding breakfast, your mama may wish to take you aside in a bid to impart some wedding-night wisdom. This will likely be very vague and full of confusing euphemisms surrounding 'the marital act' and it being 'most natural', including analogies about autumn rain and spring flowers. She may even throw in a mention of basset hounds, and all, quite masterfully, without actually informing you of the nuts (wahey!) and bolts. Persevere, dearest reader, all will become clear. Mainly because the rake you have married is very much not an innocent and will show you what's what.

ASSOCIATING WITH AN EXPECTANT

Despite what Lady Featherington may advise her daughters, I am pleased to tell all young ladies reading this that the condition of gestation is not catching. Coming into contact with a round-wombed lady, be she married or not, will not result in you falling into the same state. But mothers should beware about allowing their daughters to cavort with fallen women, as physicians are all agreed that questionable morals *are* contagious.

YOUR FIRST FORAYS INTO THE STICKY WORLD OF LOVEMAKING

Discover these rites of passage, dear reader, as you embark on coitus introitus.

FANTASY

You've watched him lick spoons for Regency England, fantasised about him 'after dark' in the bedchamber and your hands even got to first base while critiquing paintings at the RA (none of the Duke's need to be skied, for the record). Even though you were not courting this gentleman at the time, he gives you instruction for some self-love later that evening (rather forward, you might say). At first, you have not the faintest notion as to what he means. But when you retire that evening, you remember his words (and his nice face, and spoon-licking) and follow his step-by-step tutorial. Bingo – a whole new world may open up for a lady, so vivid and revelatory it inspired a pianoforte composition later, used to entertain the whole family (weird).

FINALLY ALONE

Upon engagement, it may have been deemed suitable for you to have enjoyed a moment or two of privacy with your future groom, taking the air near the Thames or dancing together at a ball. Perhaps your chaperone became more relaxed, defecting to the champagne fountain, and so keeping a whole dozen paces behind you, rather than five. Naturally you adhered to the same pre-engagement standards of decorum – refraining from lusty endeavours – not least as they risked being interrupted by your brother (a passion killer if ever there was one). You may have brought your smelling salts for when the mere proximity of his raffish tailcoat and pointy leather brogues sent you wild with desire. Now that you are no longer a debutante but a married lady, there will be much alone time and with that comes many joys and also some rough and tumble. Read on for further guidance.

MAKING SPARKS FLY ON YOUR HONEYMOON

So, it's got off to a slow start (you know, that classic issue where you suspect he hates you) until he says the magic words, explaining that he burns for you (the whole do-I-repulse-him? thing was actually all a big misunderstanding and he's well up for this marriage lark). So how does one get the ball (ahoy!) rolling?

When igniting the flame for honeymoon hook-ups, keep in mind:

FOREPLAY: Your new groom will be so good at conjugal relations that either no (or barely any) foreplay will be necessary. He'll be straight in there. And out again. Quickly.

CLOTHING AND UNDERGARMENTS: For impromptu sex, you must become adept at managing your vast layers of fabric and restrictive undergarments. For it is no good if he wishes to take you by surprise and your pantaloons are unyielding. He has long been skilled at unbuttoning his breeches, so no worries there.

SIDE BOOB: Show this as much as possible when engaged in the act of lovemaking. Gentlemen get to see your front-on knocker profile day in, day out, thanks to the wonders of the empire line (refer to Chapter 3), so offering them a side angle is a real teat. I mean, treat.

Rack up as many locales as possible:

- *The inn:* OK, you weren't expecting to be holed up in an inn for your first evening as a married lady, but there's a fire burning (literally in the hearth as well as in your loins) and your new husband goes full-frontal.

- *Against a tree:* Your coachman will be watching here, so if you like an audience this should be high on your list. Downside: tree-bark friction burns.
- *Al desco:* After a long day at work for an aristocrat, considering duchy crop rotations and how to further exploit the hoi polloi tenants, pre-dinner desk sex is just the ticket. Quills and parchment everywhere.
- *Boxing match:* A surprisingly sensual atmosphere may inspire you to engage in an exhibition of your own. The earth will move here (literally – your sex chamber is precariously positioned under the boxing ring).
- *Library ladder:* A ladder is an excellent prop, but this position takes coordination and a strong frame. Fortunately, as you're both teenagers you naturally have the strength and agility to pull this off. This will get so steamy, you will lose a satin slipper.
- *Staircase:* A good one to pull out of the bag if you haven't been speaking in a while. Moody vibes are hot. Let him attend to your lady garden (it's not all selfless) while you steady yourself by holding onto an impressively ornate bannister. Don't give a moment's thought to any servants who may be ascending the staircase, fretting about chores. They have seen it all at this stage and the carnality is now tedious to them.

DISCREET WAYS TO DISPOSE OF SEED

Siring an heir may be on the agenda for most gentleman who wish to future-proof their legacy, but for some, due to convoluted threats made when visiting their father's deathbed, they must ensure the opposite happens. Their bride must remain barren and in the dark about such anatomical matters (she may wonder if it hurts), thinking this a practice all gentlemen incorporate into the marital act. So how can a gentleman ensure discretion with bodily fluids when he reaches his 'crescendo'?

- The inn boudoir bedside (the inn keeper is used to nefarious practices and is a dab hand with a sponge).
- On top of stone steps (preferably in the rain, which will help with the clean-up).
- Into his cravat. Simple but effective.
- Onto a picnic blanket (observed by swans).
- Released into the desk drawer (a man servant can sort it out later).
- Into a first edition in the library. Just avoid that particular read in the future.

(BTW, the pull-out method is famously unreliable – gentlemen, be warned.)

UNDERCARRIAGE WELLBEING

Your lady garden has been getting a real workout of late. You've been noticing it's a little sensitive and you've been trying to stifle your crotch scratching at elegant social occasions. It's burning while on the chamber pot and you ask yourself whether that's normal. My dear lady, if your foof isn't on fire by week two of your honeymoon, something has gone awry and you need to get on it (by 'it' I mean him) post haste.

WILD BOHEMIAN ARTY ORGY ETIQUETTE

Should you find yourself in a marriage that allows each other certain 'freedoms', read on. Otherwise skip ahead to the next chapter and do not defile the virtues of your eyes by absorbing this.

You turn up to an evening soirée, bottle of claret in hand, expecting a merry evening, though not a late one (you haven't gone *out* out). Maybe there'll be some Stilton? But on arrival, you're greeted with nude women posing as Aphrodite-like statues on podiums and others prancing and waving fine silks in a most enticing manner –

yes, it really is 'a far cry from Somerset House'. It's not the evening you'd anticipated.

We've all been there. The opium pipes are cracked out, gentlemen are canoodling with other gentlemen, ladies are being openly ravished on the sumptuous oak staircase. There's not a scrap of cheese anywhere. Then it turns into a wild orgy, aka a meeting of 'like-minded souls'. How to play this curveball?

- Take care of crevices. Paint is more difficult to remove from some places than others.

- Don't reach out for your glass of brandy without looking first. Dens of depravity are full of surprises.
- Fortune favours the brave. Let go of any inhibitions – leave them at the door of the stuffy RA where they belong.
- When you bump into an orgy partner while out in polite society, say, at a picnic, be cool.
- Syphilis: this is the one thing not to take with you to (or take away from) the par-tay.

Dearest newlywed, I hope this will be a romping time of exploration. You are no longer an innocent but a lady of high society who knows a thing or two about the world. You are permitted to skip on to Chapter 7 for a further understanding of what these honeymoon frolics may lead to in the near future. *Spoiler alert*: there'll be a four-poster bed, candles and lots of writhing around, sweating and yelping (sounds nice, does it not?). 'Yaas!' you might think, but your mama will also be there. 'What?' That's right, your detailed guide to childbirth coming up.

7

MARRIAGE AND CHILDREN: A LIFE SENTENCE OR ONE'S HAPPILY EVER AFTER?

Whether you've married for love before the season is out or to avoid reputational ruin (a reason as good as any), the deed is done and wifey-lifey is about to get started. Take heed, dear bride, and listen to the words of a duchess who has been there and acquired the wedding-list Wedgwood. Though you have achieved the sole purpose of your young life to date, now is not the time to rest on your laurels. Your new raison-d'être is bearing children and in turn marrying them off. There is much to learn as a young wife, so allow me to hold your gloved hand through these uncharted waters.

KEEP THE SPARK ALIVE

This author knows a thing or two about how to succeed in (read: endure) a marriage and one never really knows what goes on inside another's household.
Do you and your groom have what it takes to go the distance? Will your branches grow together mighty as an oak or apart as fungal rot takes hold? Follow my marriage hacks to give yourselves the best chance of happiness.

MYSTERY: At times, in private, you may be permitted to address each other by your first names. Keep these instances to a minimum and they must certainly not be used in public. Defer instead to your titles, such as Viscount, Your Grace or Your Royal Highness, as appropriate. A level of formality can help keep the allure intact.

INTIMACY: Once the honeymoon is over, it is customary for the bride and groom to set up separate bedchambers. Keep the flame burning with regular night-time visits, retreating back to your private wing afterwards. Watching him scratch his scrotum in his sleep once he's passed out after an athletic lovemaking session is a vajayjay repellent.

COMMUNICATE: Keep the lines of connection open – being (somewhat) honest and vulnerable in a marriage is important. If, for example, you are under the impression he's sterile and he falsely assumes you know how babies are made and are therefore all good with him spunking into a flannel, then you're destined for a comms fail. And this can take its toll.

DATE NIGHT: Push the boat out at least once a day and enjoy quality time over a candlelit seven-course banquet, using the family's finest silverware.

DON'T ASK, DON'T TELL: Allow each other certain 'freedoms'. It can be fortuitous to adopt particular aspects of marital estrangement and a certain distance may afford you some benefits (see page 91 for orgy etiquette). This is precisely why you own both town and country estates.

A COLLECTION OF MARRIED LADIES

This is your new crew. The ball and chains of the Ton's most illustrious (and nefarious) gentlemen. As the most notable, newest bride on the scene, you will be invited to a soirée for married ladies and this author would encourage you to graciously accept the invitation. Though you may think it sounds like a dreary old engagement, mixing with a stuffy set over black tea and embroidery, how wrong you are. On arrival you will realise it is, in fact, a den of disrepute – in all of the best ways. Card games, gambling winnings, gin, pipe-smoking and general raucous times await. Chances are you'll be sitting next to someone who has only the night before had a threesome with your brother – that's fine! After two glasses of punch you'll be asking for the sordid details.

AN HEIR AND A SPARE

Your queen will enquire regularly as to your endeavours in the procreation department and will not be satisfied until an heir is born (this should be within one year of your nuptials; any later and she – and the Ton – will question your devotion to the Crown, as enjoying any benefits of being child-free is most treasonous). You are so young, you have at least twenty years of potential childbearing ahead of you (if you survive the birth, that is), so pace yourself. Remember, your first-born son will inherit the estate. The second sons get to have all the fun without the responsibility, so put your efforts into the older one (ideal traits include: being serious yet frivolous, conflicted and impetuous yet emotionally unavailable), and don't waste your time on the others. See page 113 for nourishment to quicken the womb.

YOUR GUIDE TO CHILDBIRTH

Felicitations, dearest reader, you have fulfilled your conjugal duties and spawned progeny, ensuring the posterity of your great name. Study these notes to prepare yourself for the birthing ordeal that awaits.

Have as many people present at the birth as the lying-in room will allow. They may pace outside the room getting drunk or choose to wander in and out when bored, to see how your cervix is progressing. Ensure there are no new-fangled ideas about sanitation – these are 'foreign'

notions and unpatriotic. There will be no need for anyone to wash their hands, particularly medical attendants who are permitted to rummage about your birth canal even if they have just come from a butchery dissection. Similarly, instruments such as forceps used for the previous lambing season may be reprised – any livestock debris remnants are a bonus.

A chap in a wig will guide your baby through the birth canal. He will shout 'Push!' with annoyance. Eventually you will be delivered of a child. Remember the following golden rules:

TRY NOT TO DIE: This is one of the most important things you can do during childbirth. If you have survived, read on.

CONFINEMENT: Remain horizontal for at least twenty-one days after the birth. Have the windows sealed in your bedchamber, for even a glimpse of light or inhalation of fresh air could be enough to entice puerperal fever and finish you off.

PAPA KNOWS BEST: It's customary for the father to demand to know the baby's sex long before he enquires after the mother's wellbeing. It is widely accepted as being more important to birth a son and die than to survive but birth a daughter. Once you have brought at least three males into the world, you may be permitted to bear a girl-child.

SUSTENANCE: As soon as the child emerges, it shall be fed a slice of bread soaked in water by a man-midwife. As a lady of high standing, it is imperative you do not let the child suckle from your breast (a disgusting habit that is rampant among the ill-bred of Whitechapel). If the infant refuses this starchy carb, pass it to a wet nurse. A further benefit of a milk wench is that by halting one's own lactation production, one's fertility will return with haste and you can quickly get back to the job of breeding. Nanny will then take over and you will be reunited with your child some years later, when they are more civilised.

Carry out this birthing practice every twelve to eighteen months for the next two decades (or until your demise during one of these events).

THE BABY-NAME GAME

When naming your infant, follow the alphabet as the initial letter for each successive sibling. Here are some winning baby boy and girl names – do not deviate from this list when naming your child:

A	Adon-laydon	**N**	Nedwig
B	Bebenezer	**O**	Octonaut
C	Clive	**P**	Perciveg
D	Dilldardo	**Q**	Quetta
E	Effodosia	**R**	Retzalania
F	Fanny	**S**	Sportense
G	Gaylord	**T**	Tillicentsia
H	Hyman	**U**	Uranus
I	Izeledon	**V**	Vivangela
J	Jacquiltit	**W**	Wilburfluff
K	Kiffifoots	**X**	Xmanza
L	Lubertha	**Y**	Yoghurt
M	Marmaduke	**Z**	Zebedee

PARENTING 101

What kind of parent will you be? Strict and overbearing? Distracted and negligent? Or indulgent and permissive? There are many dilemmas facing a Regency parent and decisions that have to be taken – choosing a suitable governess, arranging a good marriage or hiding the paternity of illegitimate offspring – which all take much consideration. One thing every parent is in agreement on is that after the birth, the child will be handed over to Nanny and you will be formerly reintroduced when said infant is approximately seven years old.

Take inspiration from some of the most notable parents of the Ton, who each offer their own unique take on the role. Below are their attributes and ranking.

LADY VIOLET BRIDGERTON: Laissez-faire doesn't do this style justice. A romantic soul, she desires to see her children achieve love matches (while maintaining the highest standards of pedigree, of course). She generally avoids over-meddling in her children's romantic affairs (she is even pleased when her daughter turns down a Prussian prince to slum it with a duke), is fairly chillaxed about her eldest son siphoning off family funds to put his mistress up in a flat across town, is too jaded to dish out discipline at the rowdy dining table and enjoys getting liquored up at parties from time to time (and why not? She's earned it). When she does intervene, she gives admonishments using bizarre analogies and advice, all through the elusive vehicle of metaphor. Let's give it up for this single mama. **8/10**

LADY PORTIA FEATHERINGTON: More tenacious than an unkempt wisteria in late spring, they don't come pushier than this matriarch. She'll stop at nothing to see her daughters married off, but with little help from her dowry-squandering wastrel of a husband, is it any wonder she needs to be goal-orientated? She's full of schemes, entrapping young suitors in the hope of avoiding scandal, and even finds the time to give an occasional tour of the lows and lows of London slum life. And despite her ruses almost always having disastrous outcomes, she perseveres – determination! Her waist was once the size of an orange and a half, and naturally she wants the same achievement for her daughters – and she's willing to cut off their blood circulation to do so. **4/10**

THE LATE DUKE OF HASTINGS: An old-school approach, you might say; this dad is hard to please. Nothing seems to be good enough for him – not even his son's prodigious riding and fencing prowess. He's not averse to using a hairbrush to thrash a toddler, enjoys a good name-calling session (bantz!) and even tells people his heir has died in childhood. A different approach to parenting, it's true, but perhaps there's something to be learned from this tough-love technique? (I mean, his son turned out OK. Kind of.) **2/10**

LADY DANBURY: Not actually the Duke's mama, but since he's pretty much orphaned, she steps up to the plate, *in loco parentis*. Doubling up as a child psychologist, she's a dab hand at treating infant speech impediments and instilling confidence. Part matchmaking mentor, part life coach, she's soft in the right moments but a ball breaker, too, who isn't afraid to deliver a cutting reproach exactly when needed. And she sports a top hat better than any gentleman in the Ton. **9/10**

Well, dear reader, as the season draws to a conclusion, you will attend the final ball triumphant as you are a newlywed (or at the very least engaged) – and having secured a suitable match, you shall enjoy your grand finish. And what is to happen after the London residences are boarded up and all the great families have taken their leave for their countryside retreats? Will it be matrimonial bliss or a trial to be tolerated? If you are fortunate, you will make it to old age together, a happy and fruitful union living long (well, into your late thirties or early forties) and produce many children (with hope, mostly male) to secure your legacy.

Read on to discover recipes and crafts that will help you flourish in married life.

8

RECIPES AND CRAFTS

ood. As you'll recall, you won't be having much
of this during your opening season as you must
remain as lean as a fencing sword in order to score,
but that doesn't mean that gentlemen callers don't
need to be fed, so read on for these crucial recipes that
Cook will need in her repertoire. And of course, once
you are wed you will be lady of your own household
(with the servitude of at least a dozen staff, needless to
say). Study this manual carefully so that when you are
a wife, you will have the knowledge to instruct your
servants as to how you wish to dine.

In addition, be sure to follow carefully my sage
advice on fine arts and design accomplishments.
Enjoy crafternoons with other ladies and delight in
sending gentlemen wild with lust over your
embroidery compositions.

RECIPES

Read on for the most important recipes you will rely upon, first as a debutante striving to impress and then as a married lady. These recipes are crucial for successfully brandishing your superior social status (through the medium of baked goods).

WARM MILK

One of the most notoriously difficult recipes to perfect – the most esteemed chefs on the Continent train for years in Paris to master this. Do not attempt this Herculean task alone; it needs at least two people to share the load.

You will need:

• Milk

It is essential when warming milk to place the said milk over a heat source (do ensure you use a saucepan – I once made the mistake of pouring the milk directly into the stove, and it did not end well). Attempt to light the stove.

It has proved far too complex. You are now left with only two options: drink cold milk or wake the servants.

BISCUITS

If there's one thing a hot-blooded, virile young suitor loves, it's a biscuit. When a gentleman caller comes a-knocking, Cook had better be on the case with these, quick-smart. A good biscuit could mean the difference between a proposal (being inspired by a buttery base) and a scornful rejection (too soft, no snap).

You will need:

- Flour
- Animal fat
- Sugar

Mix everything together in a large bowl and roll into a dough. Roll out into six-dozen biscuits (young men have large appetites). Cook must stamp them with the family crest, which includes your ancestral motto: *Cum laude*.

SEXY SPOON-CARESSING ICE CREAM

An essential recipe for when you need cheering up – pass
this dessert to a high-ranking hottie and observe as they
caress the spoon. Behold as the gentleman submerges the
silverware into his mouth, past his luscious lips, repeatedly
rotating it so every single drop is ravished before your
eyes. The spoon should be turned over and licked again
many times, even though the cold dessert has long been
ingested. Repeat over and over. Deposit this memory in
the bank for 'after dark', where you may pretend you are
the spoon.

You will need:

- Ice cream
- Silver spoon

Have this gentleman served ice cream (and plenty of it) in
a large bowl but with a tiny spoon (for maximum and
repeated spoon-to-tongue action).

KIPPERS ON RYE

The secret to successful conception (in addition to actually performing the marital act; refer to Chapter 6 if already married) is this life-enhancing dish.

You will need:

- Kippers
- Rye bread

Your household's smallest child servant should be responsible for bringing in the daily catch (their tiny hands are adept at entrapping these slippery creatures). The infant labourer will return to the kitchen to pass Cook the delicacy, which will be smoked over hog-infused charcoal kindling. Serve with rye bread that resembles lead and swallow all the kipper bones for a delightful textural experience. Consume twice daily during the breeding window.

IMPRESS WITH A PINEAPPLE

A fruity guest of honour – no ball is complete without a pineapple on display, which will show your vast wealth and hostess-with-the-mostess generosity.

You will need:

- **A pineapple**

Your pineapple should take pride of place on the buffet table for all to admire. Crucially, it is not for eating, but for adoration only.

WEDDING CAKE

Lavish and extravagant – the more tiers you have on your wedding cake, the higher the place in society you occupy. As a guide, you should be aiming for at least fourteen. The icing must be pure white – off-white means you're wanton.

You will need:

- Flour
- Dried fruits
- Lard
- Spices
- Golden goose eggs
- Elder wine

Have your strongest kitchen wench mix the ingredients in the kitchen's largest copper bowl. She must stir the mix an even number of rotations to ensure a long and fruitful marriage (an odd number will result in misery and adultery). If she is of simple mind and cannot count, she must be supervised.

SUGARED ALMONDS

These romantic offerings will be served at every wedding breakfast throughout the Ton, as a delicate symbol of love and fidelity.

You will need:

- The finest Persian almonds
- Icing sugar

Sprinkle the almonds with the sugar. Allow six per guest and observe how one wedding begets another.

CLYVEDON PIG

Clyvedon boasts the most succulent pork in the county, on account of the annual pig beauty pageant held at the village fair – the lucky beast is then slaughtered and the owner wins the contract to provide the Duke and Duchess of Hastings with pork products for a whole year. Get in. Should one find oneself in receipt of a slain creature, why not …?

- Invite the Ton for a hilariously ironic barn dance at your country estate and enjoy a hog roast.
- Celebrate an occasion of all-night lovemaking by welcoming the dawn with a bacon sarnie.
- Play hide the sausage.

WHOLE SUCKLING PIG ON A BED OF APPLES

Just a midweek, no-fuss banquet comprised of at least a dozen side dishes laid on exquisite silver platters with the star of the show being a whole suckling pig.

You will need:

- Clyvedon pig (see above)

Glaze the piglet with something shiny to make it look extra creepy. Make the ears of the pig extra prominent by propping them up with toothpicks. *Bon appétit!*

FALLEN WOMAN TEA

This is a tonic you should never need to imbibe, being a lady of the highest repute. However, it is important to have knowledge of it should another lady you are acquainted with need your assistance (after which you must sever all ties with this Jezebel). This recipe is not something Cook can rustle up; it must be kept the utmost secret (the help being terrible gossips who lack discretion).

You will need:

- Juniper berries
- Dandelion root
- Dried spices
- Dried rose petals
- Boiling water

Pound the dry ingredients with a pestle and mortar, while looking anxious and aggravated (this part is important to impart flavour). Add to a fine china teacup with saucer (one may be dealing with a fallen woman but one still has standards). Pour over the boiling water and infuse. Drink. Collapse.

HANGOVER CURES

It's very important never to admit to overindulging or having any form of sherry dependence. Instead, blame it on 'a poor night's sleep' or something you ate. Here are some tonics that can cure the ills on the morning after the night before.

RAW EGGS AND GARLIC

If a sup or ten have been taken, this is the ultimate remedy to have you back promenading and bashing out the tunes on the pianoforte in no time. It is important you use one clove of garlic for every tipple you have imbibed, swallowing the cloves whole.

You will need:

- Ostrich eggs
- Garlic

Whisk two eggs with the appropriate number of cloves (see above) of garlic.

Open wide – down the hatch.

MACKEREL AND BURNT TOAST

Your gentleman has been propping up the tavern and brawling in Mayfair until the early hours – what japes! Delight him with this delicious breakfast that Cook will rustle up. It is long said that oil and coals soak up any lingering gut hooch.

You will need:

- Burnt toast
- Mackerel

First, prepare the toast – hurl some bread in the fire grate until the kitchen is smoking. Fry the mackerel. Place the mackerel on top of the toast. *Voilá.*

You may need to force-feed the rake in question.

A SHARPENER OF RUM

Hair of the dog – consume this before you have even left your bedchamber.

You will need:

- Rum

Bottoms up.

ROUGE (FOR YOUR SPLENDID FACE – DO NOT EAT)

A hangover cure for the visage. Your lady's maid will be able to manufacture a variety of cosmetics combining tinctures from the apothecary as well as the secret ingredient: arsenic. This miraculous element works wonders on the complexion and has basically no side effects (apart from the occasional death).

You will need:

- Candle wax
- Dried rose petals
- Bergamot oil
- Arsenic

Mix all the components together. Have your maid apply this blush sparingly to the cheekbones for an instant pick-me-up to treat a complexion battered from quaffing. If you are feeling daring, apply to the collar bones.

CRAFTS

As a refined Regency lady, you will be highly
accomplished at a variety of delicate feminine crafts. These
attributes will count in your favour with your suitors, who
monitor your accomplishments and tot them up on little
score cards they keep in their tailcoat. They then compare
these scores among the ladies they are courting in order to
assess superiority; for example, Lady Cornelia Pilkinghat
speaks French *and* Italian, and can also cross-stitch the
Greek alphabet blindfolded, but Lady Sybil Syphilis-
Thwaite can play the lute, construct a net purse in a single
evening *and* is not merely a fine horsewoman but can ride
a mule with considerable talent, too. Decisions, decisions.

MAKE AN IMPACT WITH YOUR EMBROIDERY

As a refined lady, your sewing expertise must be
top-drawer. Obviously you will never use these skills for
practical 'work' (as that is all your maid's domain –
similarly, leave the needlework of caps and handkerchiefs
to the hags of the middle classes). Instead, you will be
using a needle as a decorative medium, to embroider the
finest detailing onto small pieces of mystery fabric. Take

your projects with you when paying calls or use the time while you are in your carriage to perfect your technique (just take care – needles and potholes are not a happy mix and ladies have been known to embroider their noses when jolted in their landau).

Keep in mind my needlework instructions, which will all stand to you when husband-hawking:

- Silhouette crafting – embroider your profile onto the finest lace, slimming down any jowls or double chin. Gift this to your favourite suitor so that he may be reminded of your great beauty (well, outline). This is particularly helpful if your complexion leaves a lot to be desired.
- Ensure your decorative skills are fancy indeed, using gold threads on your fabric panels when sewing your silhouette.

- Whether you're pining after a particular suitor or recently betrothed, practise sewing your would-be new title and initials into fine muslins and weave these around tulips (which, as we know from Lady Bridgerton, represent passion).
- Running stitch – this author regrets to inform you that if one's stitching is a battleground, you're en route to spinsterhood. Keep it neat.

When embroidering for your admirer, be sure to consider the coded messages that your needlework could convey. Here are a few sample patterns that you may wish to try, which will be sure to get him hot under his oversized collar:

THE ART OF FLOWER-PRESSING

Ideally the flowers you press will have been sent to you by a suitor and you are committing them to romantic posterity by squashing them flat. Obtain the two largest, most weighty volumes in the library and crush the delicate blooms between them. Display these pressings around the drawing room, subtly bringing them to the attention of any other suitors who call.

KNITTING OR CROCHETING

What are you – a pauper? A lady of fashion should never debase herself with so functional a pastime.

WHAT YOUR HANDWRITING SAYS ABOUT YOU

Perfecting one's quillwork is a most becoming pastime for a young lady. Once you embark on married life, your letter-writing frequency will increase as you will need to inscribe acceptances to invitations to grand occasions far and wide – and also write long letters to your single friends to boast about them. It is, therefore, very important that you give a good impression through your quill work, especially as your hidden flaws and weaknesses are easily revealed through your hand.

Pay heed to the below – if your writing exhibits any of these traits, you may never get past debutante stage (shudder).

- *Frilly lettering:* You're a silly girl who needs a good talking to.
- *Loose lettering = loose morals:* Mind those gaps.
- *Slanting to the right:* You're an animal in the sack, congratulations.
- *Slanting to the left:* Your sass may get you in trouble one day soon.
- *Sloppy dotting:* A lady who cannot fastidiously dot her 'i's and 'j's will never be a successful mistress of a prominent household.

PAINTING

Another excellent opportunity to convene with gentlemen is to arrange a hillside painting excursion. Painting *en plein air* may allow you a few extra steps of freedom away from your chaperone and in the company of eligible honeys.

Begin with sketching your environment – gentlemen will observe your way with a pencil as it gives insight into the quality of your overall education. Be mindful that they wish you to be learned but not too clever (a wife who is too clever uncovers all their wrongdoings). Remember, it's accomplishment over education, so you may need to feign half-wittedness (again, strike a balance here – go too far and it is the asylum for you). Choose a picturesque, romantic setting and show off your paintbrush prowess by capturing the natural beauty and light of the scene (be careful that your trees do not resemble phallic shapes or the gentlemen will think you the wrong sort). Your servants shall pack a picnic of the finest foods and wines – what larks one will have!

GIFT BASKETS FOR SERFS

Once you are married and have ladyship over an estate, remember the little people, the tenant farmers who enable you to live off the fat of the land. Obviously you will keep their rents tripled, but to soften the blow, bring them a gift basket once a decade with treats from their master's estate.

You will need:

- **Lavender**
- **Honey**
- **Bread**

Shock your housekeeper by picking some lavender from the gardens yourself. Your lady's maid will come with you and do most of the picking and bunching while you chat mindlessly.

Do not attempt to harvest your own honey, for that is a step too far – though you are intrepid, this would be quite mad. Have a domestic drudge cultivate the honeycomb for you (if you are feeling generous, you may allow him to wear a protective suit).

Add the lavender, honey and bread to a pretty wicker basket to give to any natives (deduct the cost of the basket from their annual tithes – you are not a charity, after all).

Dearest reader, your scholarship in groom-hunting is nearing completion, but I implore you to read on and complete the scientific tests that follow, which draw on empirical research that will match you to your perfect companion (if you have not found him already).

9

PARLOUR GAMES

Move over cribbage and whist! Here are some games to play with one's chums.

ARE YOU THERE, WHISTLEDOWN?

Should you have mislaid your duelling pistols, this is your next best opportunity to defend your honour. This sophisticated demonstration of skill relies on quick wits and the reflexes of a cat. Your weapon is a rolled-up edition of Lady Whistledown's most recent bulletin. Two players will 'duel' at a time. Ensure you choose your opponent carefully – the larger the grudge you hold, the better your chances for success.

You must both be blindfolded, then lie on your fronts on the floor of a grand drawing room, with a little space between you. The villain you are playing against will call to you, '*Are you there, Whistledown?*' while holding the paper weapon, then when you answer they will attempt to thrash you (swine!). You must use your wiles to avoid this blow, and if you do, it will be your turn to beat the libertine! Draw your paper roll high above your head and use all your might to swing for them. If you are victorious, they must grant you the deeds to their home, along with their finest thoroughbred.

PIN THE SIDEBURNS ON THE DUKE

The perfect diversion for a young debutante at her hen party – is there a better way to bid farewell to one's single days than enjoying an evening of disrepute (with parlour games)?

Commission a large canvas oil painting of the husband-to-be, which should then be positioned on an easel. Place a blindfold around the eyes of each competitor in turn and spin her around until she turns pale green and is about to throw up. Place a caterpillar in both of her hands and observe with merriment how she stumbles about like a drunk and attempts to deposit the insect on the portrait. Repeat with all in attendance. The winner is the person who most accurately pins the caterpillars to the chops of the Duke.

LORD FEATHERINGTON'S CAT

Sit with your chums in a circle and take it in turns to describe the notorious feline that roams Mayfair and belongs to the rogue Lord Featherington, using descriptions that follow the alphabet. Allow me to give an example:

A   Lord Featherington's cat has a protruding *anus*.
B   Lord Featherington's cat is a *brute* of a cat.
C   Lord Featherington's cat has *camel toe*.

Make this game more interesting by using your pocket watch to give each player a mere five seconds to think of a characteristic. Consuming port while playing will help

with the tedium from the letter G onwards (twenty-six letters can make this game a rather slow burn). When Lord Featherington plays, naturally he likes to place a wager on the outcome. Which he then loses.

Miaow!

BRIDGERTON BINGO

This chart should be drawn up and placed somewhere conspicuous for the evening. Any time one of the present company unwittingly performs the action on that square, their initials should be drawn inside the square. The first person to tick off six squares on the bingo board pays for the next trip to the ice-cream parlour!

If any player completes the entire board of an evening, they must go straight to the kitchen and assist with the washing-up. (NB 'Washing up' is something servants must do after meals to ensure all the dishes are clean. This author doesn't know anyone to have done it, but she believes they lick them clean or rinse them in the rain.)

Says the word 'Splendid'	Takes a turn about the room	Has an emotional outburst	A hair falls out of place
Plays one too many pieces on the pianoforte	Talks about their horse	Gossips	Licks their spoon unnecessarily
Looks broodingly into the fire/ out the window	Suggests a visit to Bath	Is exceedingly ashamed of their conduct	Mentions a ball
Misunder-stands something	Fingers their jewels/cravat	Says something is of 'great import'	Swoons into someone's arms

CHARADES

A wonderful opportunity to practise your acting skills and ridicule your family, friends and neighbours at the same time. Divide your party into two teams. In turns, a member of the opposite team will give you the name of a topical cultural offering. Speaking not a word, you must mime these artistic works for your team members to interpret. A pocket watch will signal when your time is up.

For example, you might be tasked with performing one of the below:

OPERAS: Beethoven's *Fidelio* or Rossini's *Tancredi*.

BOOKS: Hot-off-the-press *Pride and Prejudice*, the dreary old Book of Common Prayer or Fordyce's *Sermons*, or why not try your hand at *Erotica for the Regency Lady*? (Do not undertake this charade if playing with family.)

MUSIC: Handel's *Messiah* (this author assures you charades will be more fun than actually listening to this oratorio) or one of the songs that seem to delight the plebs, such as 'The Yellow Hair'd Laddie'.

FICTIONARY

Borrow the dictionary from your papa's vast library and have some quills and parchment at the ready. Select one person to act as dictionary chief and distribute the writing material among the rest of your party. The chief will select an obscure word from the dictionary (that no one in the room will be familiar with – certainly not the ladies, who are uneducated) and privately write down its true meaning. Each player must then write a believable interpretation of the word on their paper, without allowing anyone else to see it. The chief will then gather the 'definitions' and read them in turn to the group (along with the genuine meaning) and each player must vote for the definition they believe to be accurate, scoring a point for every one they guess correctly.

For example:

SNOLLYGOSTER

- A vexing infection of the snout, which causes mucus build-up and general agitation.
- A shrewd, unprincipled person, especially a politician.
- A particularly loud sneeze that involuntarily expels a modicum of urine.
- The piercing that some men have in their nether regions.

GYASCUTUS

- A gynaecological condition resulting in a burning, prickling sensation.
- The act of congress atop a cantering horse. Named for the Roman senator who was renowned for performing this trick in public.

- When one's eyes bulge perceptibly from the sockets after suffering a shock.
- A large, imaginary four-legged beast with legs on one side longer than the other for walking on hillsides.

TITTYNOPE

- A small quantity left over, such as the dregs at the bottom of a cup.
- A facial expression that communicates unequivocally that one's bottom is not a playground.
- A spell used in an Ancient Egyptian burial ritual.
- When one's breasts escape from their corset jail.

CUDDLE-ME-BUFF

- Embrace me unclad by breeches.
- A home that boasts the shiniest knobs and knockers in the Ton.
- Beer!
- An athletic type, whose physique is so impressive it leaves one feeling inadequate and in need of an embrace.

And now, dear reader, it is the moment you've been waiting for. It is time to complete some quizzes that will reveal your true self as well as your innermost desires.

10

QUIZZES

Dearest reader, complete these examinations into the soul with the utmost concentration and uncover your innermost desires. Each quiz will reveal deep-seated insight into the strengths and weaknesses of your character, as well as what you are truly seeking in life (spoiler: a wealthy husband).

DISCOVER YOUR REGENCY TITLE

If I depend solely upon future princesses, duchesses or ladies to purchase this book, my publisher reliably informs me that my earnings shall be slim indeed. And so, for the gratification of the rabble dreaming of marrying a duke or viscount, here is a scientific method to determine what your title might have been had you succeeded – in an alternate reality where you were of any significance.

MONTH OF BIRTH

January/February	Lady
March/April	Duchess
May/June	Marquess
July/August	Baroness
September/October	Countess
November/December	Viscountess

FIRST INITIAL

A	Fangle-	H	Colly-
B	Wobble-	I	Bumber-
C	Bridge-	J	Flibber-
D	Whistle-	K	Timber-
E	Feathering-	L	Tanning-
F	Gubbin-	M	Wibble-
G	Widder-	N	Snolly-

O	Bibble-	U	Lucken-
P	Hawks-	V	Sauce-
Q	Pember-	W	Buckle-
R	Farting-	X	Manning-
S	Rattle-	Y	Mont-
T	Penning-	Z	Sore-

LAST INITIAL

A	-berry	N	-brook
B	-down	O	-bill
C	-sley	P	-well
D	-ville	Q	-skit
E	-spittle	R	-son
F	-loo	S	-cock
G	-wample	T	-field
H	-diddle	U	-bling
I	-shins	V	-chard
J	-fuzzle	W	-joy
K	-snee	X	-whistle
L	-borough	Y	-shaw
M	-ton	Z	-gill

STAR SIGN

ARIES	of Cumberland
TAURUS	of Berkshire
GEMINI	of Staffordshire
CANCER	of Clancarty
LEO	of Gloucestershire
VIRGO	of Worcestershire
LIBRA	of Nottinghamshire
SCORPIO	of Warwickshire
SAGITTARIUS	of Lincolnshire
CAPRICORN	of Norfolk
AQUARIUS	of Anglesey
PISCES	of Marlborough

WHICH SEXY BRIDGERTON HERO IS YOUR TRUE LOVE?

Are you destined to marry a prince or a pauper? There's only one way to find out.

WHAT IS YOUR IDEA OF THE PERFECT DATE?

- **A** A chaperoned promenade in the park (1)
- **B** A chaperoned ball (2)
- **C** A chaperoned conversation in the drawing room (3)
- **D** A chaperoned garden party (4)
- **E** A threesome at an artists' party (5)

WHAT'S THE MOST IMPORTANT QUALITY YOU LOOK FOR IN A HUSBAND?

- **A** Epic dance moves (1)
- **B** A crown (2)
- **C** A good left hook (3)
- **D** Massive sideburns (4)
- **E** Sexual stamina (5)

WHAT'S THE BIGGEST TURN-OFF?

- **A** Not being the Duke (1)
- **B** A gambling problem (2)
- **C** Being in love with another (3)
- **D** Wanton sexual appetites (4)
- **E** Making stupid promises to his dead father (5)

WHAT OCCUPATION WOULD YOU LIKE YOUR POTENTIAL HUSBAND TO HAVE?

- **A** No occupation: he's a gentleman (1)
- **B** A prince (2)
- **C** A boxer (3)
- **D** An artist (4)
- **E** A womaniser (5)

WHAT DO YOU SEE IN YOUR FUTURE?

- **A** Living independently (1)
- **B** Debts (2)
- **C** Companionship (3)
- **D** Children (4)
- **E** Lots of sex (5)

HOW WOULD YOU GAIN THE ATTENTION OF A MAN YOU FANCY?

A Introduce yourself to him (1)
B Faint at his feet (2)
C Wear yellow (3)
D Flirt with every other man at the party (4)
E Hoick up the cleavage even further (5)

WHAT WOULD BE YOUR MAN'S DRINK OF CHOICE?

A Tea (1)
B Beer (2)
C Champagne (3)
D Whisky (4)
E Absinthe (5)

WHERE IS YOUR FAVOURITE PLACE TO MAKE LOVE?

A At the theatre (1)
B In the library (2)
C In a pavilion (3)
D On a staircase (4)
E At a party (5)

WHAT WOULD BE YOUR IDEA OF A DREAM PROPOSAL?

A Through your father (1)
B At a ball (2)
C In the drawing room (3)
D With the guy pressured into it by you to cover your pregnancy (4)
E With the guy forced into it by your brother at gunpoint (5)

WHAT WOULD YOU MOST LIKE YOUR BETROTHED TO GIVE YOU?

A A poem (1)
B A new hat (2)
C A diamond ring (3)
D An orgasm (4)
E An STD (5)

Time to add up your scores and find out which of these hunks is yours!

10–14: NIGEL BERBROOKE

Now, we can all admit Nige isn't exactly the romantic hero one has been dreaming of, but he's persistent (that can be a good quality in some situations); he can be felled pretty easily with a well-aimed punch (that's useful to know); he is … he sometimes … oh, I'm sorry, dear reader, he's a creep. But you're stuck with him.

15–19: LORD FEATHERINGTON

You may be aware that Lord Featherington is a gambling addict, and, yes, that may very well mean he will drive you and your family into ruin … but would that be his fate with you? Unhappiness can send us all down the wrong path. With a bit of love and encouragement, old Featherington would probably make you a fine husband – and his match-fixing certainly shows resourcefulness, if nothing else.

20–24: SIR HENRY GRANVILLE

To any ladies determined to find fault in any situation, you may see a few here. Sir Henry Granville is unlikely to fulfil some of the requirements of a 'traditional husband', and of an evening would likely prefer the company of your brother to your own. But to a lady of a certain inclination, he might just offer you the life you've always dreamt of. As the wife of a sought-after artist, you shall not want for money, connections and … varied society. Think of the parties! In time he might just become the best friend you've never had and grow to love and cherish you in his own way. Your own extra-marital affairs will be encouraged, and you will enjoy all the benefits of being a married woman without the disadvantages that the yoke of marriage usually entails.

25-29: PRINCE FRIEDRICH

Now we're talking! Prince of Prussia, very romantic, likes kids, will take you to fun things like boxing matches, is a TOTAL gentleman and won't even reproach you if you take him on a merry dance and make him believe you're going to marry him but then drop him at the last second for a hotter duke ... I'd say he's pretty near perfect. (If you overlook the matter of the very pedestrian nature of the sex you'll be having for the rest of time.)

30-34: COLIN BRIDGERTON

Colin may not be as dashing as his older brothers – and his name is *Colin* – but he's undoubtedly the kindest man about the Ton. Declaring that he'd have been happy to marry a certain lady if she could have been honest with him, despite her carrying another's child, makes him a pretty good egg in this writer's opinion. He also has a great sense of adventure and wants to travel the world – I'd say you've got yourself a pretty good one here.

35-39: WILL MONDRICH

Humana humana (if you'll excuse my French). This sexy boxer knows what to do with his fists and respects women in a very un-Regency type way. You know you'll be in great hands with this manly yet sensitive chap, who will even put his reputation in jeopardy to make sure he can support you and the kids. Sure, he's not as rich as many of the other men on this list, but I'm confident he has ways of making up for that.

40-44: BENEDICT BRIDGERTON

This saucepot is a debauched reprobate – and this author loves it. Nude life-drawing parties that turn into mass orgies? Just your typical Saturday night out with friends. If you think you can keep up with his wanton sexual appetite, then he is your man – just expect that you may have to share him with others.

45-49: VISCOUNT ANTHONY BRIDGERTON, AKA SIDEBURNS FOR DAYS

This poor viscount is torn between love and duty – as all the best romantic heroes are. The burden of a title, assuming the role of head of the family since his dear papa died, plus having four annoying sisters he needs to find matches for – no wonder he's stressed. But now he's yours you can soothe his tormented soul and the demons he is battling. Help him lift the strain of responsibility that weighs heavily on those strong shoulders … And once you've got him between the sheets you're sure to discover that there is NOTHING weighing him down or holding him back (except maybe his sideburns).

50: SIMON BASSET, DUKE OF HASTINGS
Nice one! You've bagged the Duke! Yes, he comes with daddy issues, a penchant for bare-knuckle boxing (although somehow he comes away unmarked each time), will even risk his own life/killing his own best friend/ disappointing the love of his life to spite his deceased father … but have you seen his ass?

WHICH BRIDGERTON DEBUTANTE ARE YOU?

Discover more about what your own approach to the debutante season should be, by learning which of these famous ladies you most closely resemble.

WHAT DOES YOUR DREAM DAY LOOK LIKE?

A Making love in every room of your substantial estate.

B Throwing off your corset, letting the mullet hang loose and chain-smoking on the garden swing.

C Quietly observing what everyone else is doing, especially any misdemeanours, and jotting it all down in your notebook.

D A date in a gallery with a wealthy man, where you pretend to faint and they fall in love with you.

E Having a long lie-in, lounging in your crop top, after a wild night.

HOW DO YOU FEEL AT A PARTY?

A The belle of the ball – you're at ease but do not crave adoration.

B You were supposed to attend but thought what a waste of time, you have far better things to do (like catching up on some fem-lit).

C Totes awky momo. You watch the clock until it's a polite time to leave.

D Superior. You note what everyone is wearing and whether you've seen them in that outfit before.

E You breeze in, do one lap (maybe even sit on a lap) and bounce outta there.

IS YOUR PERFECT PARTNER ...?

A A sexy but complicated man of influence, who goes against the grain by having designer stubble when no other men would be daring enough.

B A good book.

C A jolly but steady chap.

D Anyone in a position of power or rank.

E Some raffish and troubled but adoring cad. Side-whiskers are a bonus.

WHAT IS YOUR MOST IMPRESSIVE SKILL?

A Your ability to climax after mere seconds of penetrative sex.

B Your tenacity in finding out the truth, even if you get it wrong most of the time.

C To slip under the radar with such discretion that you see and hear all.

D You do look good in a diamanté hairband, it must be said.

E You're extremely flexible, which comes in handy.

WHAT DOES YOUR FUTURE HOLD?

A Babies. Lots of cute babies.

B You plan to launch a *salon* of ideas, where you support other writers and thinkers, and generally alter society for the better.

C A very pleasant marriage, quarrel-free and content, with fortnightly missionary sex. And a secret writing career.

D Hosting smug book clubs and competitive PTA meetings.

E Singing, fun and – who knows?

RESULTS:

MOSTLY As: DAPHNE BASSET (NEÉ BRIDGERTON), DUCHESS OF HASTINGS

OK, so you may not be the biggest personality in the world but you have hidden depths. You're traditional but not prudish and a pillar of reliability in times of crisis. You're thoughtful, conscientious and pragmatic. You want everyone to get along. But underneath that cool exterior, a fire burns. This is the side to you that comes out 'after dark' (or also in the daytime in the library, on the stairs, in the study, etc.).

MOSTLY Bs: MISS ELOISE BRIDGERTON

A heroine for our times – had you been around a hundred years ago you'd have been marching with a 'Votes for Women' placard. Irreverent and open-minded, you're not afraid to question the absurdities of life and push for answers. A loyal friend – there's never a minute's peace with you around.

MOSTLY Cs: MISS PENELOPE FEATHERINGTON

Not to be underestimated, you have hidden reserves of fortitude and ingenuity. People may initially think you're a pushover but you have ways and means to get what you want and you're not averse to employing ruthlessness from time to time. Though life may seem tame when you're starting out, it's all going to come good for you.

MOSTLY Ds: MISS CRESSIDA COWPER

Urgh, go and have a long, hard look at yourself. You need taking down a peg or two.

MOSTLY Es: SIENA ROSSO

Legend. Not a debutante as such (you despair about what these ladies, who do not have an occupation, actually do to pass the time); you are making your own way in the world, and having a shagging good time while doing so. In the past you have been hurt by men, but it has only served to make you stronger and more resilient. You go, girl!

APPENDIX 1

THE GENTLEMEN CATALOGUE, 1813 SEASON

Young ladies, peruse these pages to select the hottest bachelors of the season. Ding dong. These men are among the cream of London and each would prove quite the catch on parchment, though admittedly falling in love with them may be a stretch. Should you wish to get to know any of these gentlemen, simply write to me (Lady Wibblefluffle, Fluffle House, Mayfair) and you shall be introduced at a ball where you may observe how he spins.

DUKE DILLYBOT

CURRENT RELATIONSHIP STATUS:
Depends who's asking.

INCOME:
I live off the fat of the land.

HOW WOULD YOUR FRIENDS DESCRIBE YOU?
I cannot boast many friendships.

WHAT MAKES YOU MARRIAGE MATERIAL?
I'll brush your hair and watch you sleep.

◦◦◦ EARL TONENBRIDGE ◦◦◦

WHAT ARE YOU LOOKING FOR IN A DEBUTANTE?
A large dowry. I have many debts to settle.

LIST YOUR TOP THREE HOBBIES:
Laughing at my own great jokes, collecting dolls, intercourse.

ANY ILLEGITIMATE CHILDREN?
I operate a don't-ask-don't-tell policy.

WHAT DO YOU HAVE TO OFFER A LADY?
The earldom.

∼❂ VISCOUNT WAGGLETUFF ❂∼

WHERE DO YOU SEE YOURSELF IN FIVE YEARS?
Inheriting my father's title.

TOWN OR COUNTRY?
There are more brothels in town.

WHAT WAS THE LAST BOOK YOU READ?
I'm more of a boobs than a books man.

WHAT IS YOUR SPIRIT ANIMAL?
Puss moth larva.

BARON REPTILLINGTON

WHAT DO YOU DO FOR A LIVING?
Ha! Good one.

WHAT WOULD YOUR IDEAL WEEKEND LOOK LIKE?
What's a weekend?

WHAT ARE YOUR MOST APPEALING HABITS?
I can trim my toenails with my teeth (and I keep the cuttings in a pretty little box).

WHAT WILL YOUR EPITAPH READ?
Carpe vinum.

∼⦶ LORD FORTESCUE-FRAMPTON ⦷∼

HOW WOULD YOU DESCRIBE YOURSELF?
Babe magnet.

HOW DO YOU WIND DOWN?
With my many cats.

WHAT WOULD YOU WANT A WIFE TO BRING TO THE RELATIONSHIP?
More cats.

WHY SHOULD A YOUNG LADY CHOOSE YOU?
See my first answer.

∿ VISCOUNT RATHERSPOON ∾

DESCRIBE YOUR IDEAL WOMAN.
A lady who likes to snuggle.

HOW DO YOU ACT UNDER PRESSURE?
I avoid any sort of strife or inconvenience at all costs.

WHAT IS YOUR GREATEST ACHIEVEMENT TO DATE?
Being born into privilege.

IF YOU COULD CHANGE ANYTHING ABOUT YOURSELF,
WHAT WOULD IT BE?
I should so like thicker sideburns.

∿ BARON BRACEGIRDLE ∿

WHAT IS YOUR BEST MEMORY FROM YOUR CHILDHOOD?
Breaking a china figurine and blaming it on the butler, for a lark.

DO YOU FIND IT EASY TO MAKE NEW FRIENDS?
No, I just get them on a retainer.

HOW WOULD YOUR FAMILY DESCRIBE YOU?
Probably as 'distant'. I haven't spoken to them in about ten years.

WOULD YOU RATHER READ A BOOK, WATCH AN OPERA OR PLAY A SPORT?
I'd rather peruse the balance book for my estate.

Appendix 1

∼◦ MR EVERSMALL THE YOUNGER ◦∼

WHAT WAS THE HAPPIEST TIME OF YOUR LIFE?
Without doubt when I was just a young lad, fishing in the lakes and streams about our manor, with my chums. Whether we were collecting frogspawn to scare Nanny or tiddlers to compare in the bathroom, I was never happier. I sometimes think –

WHAT TOPIC OF CONVERSATION IS OFF-LIMITS?
They say you should never discuss politics, religion or money. But as I know nothing of politics, have zip to say about church except that the vicar is a splendid chap and everyone I know is minted, I don't worry too much about those. The thing I don't think should be discussed is the amount of hair a man has upon his head. It can lead to all sorts of injured egos and sadness.

WHAT'S THE LAST THING YOU READ?
The instructions for a bottle of hair rejuvenation shampoo.

WHAT'S YOUR FAVOURITE MEAL OF THE DAY?
Breakfast. Or elevenses. Or luncheon. Or perhaps afternoon tea. But I do like dinner. And supper. And I looove a midnight feast with a truly special chum. But I'm not sure you can beat a truly excellent snack. I sometimes like to drop into the kitchen and ask Cook –

APPENDIX 2

HOW TO CALCULATE YOUR DOWRY

Dear reader, in Chapter 5 I explained the charming convention of how your father will pay another man to take you away. Your new groom may spend this legacy as he wishes – perhaps he shall invest it wisely or set part of it aside to provide for educational expenses for your future children. Or maybe he will use it in brothels or to rack up debts across town. It's really not your business. How much your father has granted for your dowry will be of great interest to suitors, though – many of whom care little for love and are all about the dollar.

Appendix 2

DOWRY MATHEMATICS

A PRINCESS: No dowry necessary here and she will likely be marrying a sibling or first cousin, so the family wealth remains in situ.

THE ELDEST DAUGHTER OF A DUKE: Ker-ching! A sizeable sum of £20,000 shall be paid to the lucky groom and within the bride's trousseau will be two diamond necklaces, one pair of emerald earrings, a ruby ring and a solid gold dagger (just in case).

THE THIRD DAUGHTER OF A BARON: £5,000 and a string of pearls – not too shabby.

THE ONLY CHILD OF A GRAY'S INN SOLICITOR: £100 per annum while her father is alive. Granted, this isn't enough to live it large every day, but it will help a middle-class (shudder) family keep the wolves from the door.

A STRONG PEASANT GIRL: One mule (her new husband shall have the mule on Tuesdays, Thursdays and Saturdays and must return it to his father-in-law for use on Mondays, Wednesday and Fridays. On Sunday, said mule will be allowed one hour off from ploughing before being rented to a neighbour).

ACKNOWLEDGEMENTS

I should like to thank all the debutantes I have known, past and present, who have given me such plentiful fodder for this book. Particularly the ones who disgraced themselves – there is often more to learn from failure than success.

I should also like to thank my husband, without whom I should never have been elevated to such a position from which I can look down upon the rest of the Ton. I do so enjoy a lofty vantage point.